30 DAYS

DISCOVERING THE POWER OF PRAYER

DREW MEYER

Copyright© 2020 by **Drew Meyer**

All rights reserved. No part of this publication may be reproduced, distributed or transmitted in any form or by any means, without prior written permission.

Printed by CreateSpace, An Amazon.com Company
Drew Meyer Press
409 13th St
Ames, IA 50010
www.livethemessage.org

Unless otherwise specified, Scripture quotations used in this book are taken from the 2016 edition of the Holy Bible, English Standard Version®, ESV®. Copyright © by Crossways Bibles, Wheaton, IL.

Scripture quotations marked NLT are from the NLT® Bible (Holy Bible, New Living Translation®. Copyright © by Tyndale House Publishers, Carol Stream, IL.

Book Layout & Design: Kayla Meyer
Front & Back Cover Design: Kayla Meyer
Back Cover Image: Paige Holzbauer & Robert Jinkins
Images: Paige Holzbauer, Robert Jinkins, Tayler Nickerson & Amy Savage

30 Days: Discovering the Power of Prayer / Drew Meyer. -- 1st ed.
ISBN: 9781689367820

Contents

Introduction	1
Instructions for the Bible Reading Plan	3
Daily Reading	
01: Discovery	6
02: Re-Imagine	8
03: Do You Have Urgency?	10
04: Do You Hear Him Knocking?	12
05: Intimacy	16
06: Identity	18
07: Purpose	22
08: God is Faithful	26
09: Running Everywhere but Getting Nowhere	28
10: God is my Strength	32
11: Fruitful	34
12: It's Not a Formula, It's the Gospel	38
13: Sons, Daughters, and Heirs	40
14: The Gospel of Grace	44
15: Authority in Christ	46
16: Keeping Promises	52
17: Genuine Faith Through a Renewed Mind	56
18: The Mystery of the Kingdom	60
19: Things Worth Fighting For	62
20: Embrace Desperation	68
21: A History of Desperation	70
22: Read It and Believe It	74
23: The Stakes are High	76
24: Why We Pray Together	80
25: The Power of Unity	82
26: An Invitation for Action	86
27: Jesus our Example	88
28: Praying in the Spirit	92
29: The Secret Place	94
30: Experience is Necessary	96
Appendix: Promises of God	99
Image Index	101
Acknowledgements	101
About the Author	103
Prayer Journal	104

Introduction

Prayer is an experience and expression of a love relationship initiated by the grace of God. Prayer is not a religious duty or a task assigned to us. Prayer is a privilege of relationship with a living, loving God. And therefore, prayer is something we do in our coming and going, and it's something we also set aside time for.

This book is intended to be a tool to inspire more gospel-centered prayer in followers of Jesus. Several years ago, as a college student, I responded to a challenge to set aside 30 days for concerted prayer. Every morning, a few friends and I would arrive at our church well before our 8am classes and we would pray for an hour. We didn't know much and didn't have much of an agenda. Our only desire was to know God in a deeper way. Over this 30 days (and the weeks following) the trajectory of my life forever changed, as I discovered for myself what it meant to walk in relationship with Jesus through prayer.

This book is inspired by that 30-day challenge I received years ago. Something significant can happen in a believer and the Church when we set aside intentional time to seek God in a fresh way. This book provides the structure for a 30-day journey so that more people can experience intimacy with God.

The ingredients for intimacy with God are: 1) His Word
    2) prayer
    3) obedience

Each of these are initiated by the grace of God. They are not ways to 'get to God', but responses to God's love and provision for us. There are many aspects or dimensions to each of these ingredients, but these basic ingredients fuel the flames of love relationship with God.

Every day of this book you will see these three ingredients providing the flow of your time with God.

You have the opportunity to discover a fresh, vibrant relationship with Jesus on a daily basis. This short, 30-day journey gets us going in the right direction and will launch us into a new trajectory of walking with God by weaving together His Word, prayer, and immediate obedience.

Instructions for the Bible Reading Plan

The Word of God plays an integral part in our life of prayer. The Word of God is the revelation of Who God is and His plan of redemption. It's through this understanding of the Word of God that we pray, not wishfully, but confidently, knowing that the God who became "God with us", truly wants to be with us in daily relationship. The Word of God is foundational.

This is why I have included a Bible Reading Plan in this 30 days of discovering the power of prayer. This Bible Reading Plan includes a few passages each day that highlight the relevant truth for that day. But, I want to make sure you are able to make the most of your time in God's Word. If you are unfamiliar with the Bible or have never opened it in a relational way, here are some helpful thoughts for you as you begin these 30 days.

The Bible is divided into two parts – Old Testament and New Testament.
The first 39 books of the Bible are the story of God's design, our rebellion, and God's plan of redemption leading up to the life of Jesus. Some of these books are difficult to understand and parts of the Old Testament are very "messy". But keep in mind that when you read in the Old Testament, central to its story is our need for a savior.

The next 27 books of the Bible are the story of God's redemption through His perfect Son, Jesus, His Church, and the Second Coming of Christ in the age to come. Many of these books emphasize God's radical mercy and grace, and give us instruction on how to live our lives in response to His grace.

The Bible is understood in context.
It's important, as much as possible, to seek understanding of Scrip-

ture passages in context. The most important context is the immediate context of the passage. What are the passages before and after saying? After that, much can be understood by knowing the context of the specific book (i.e., Matthew, Romans, or Ephesians) such as who wrote the book, why they wrote it, and who they were writing to. And finally, it's always helpful to understand the broader context within the redemptive story. Is
the passage before Jesus (i.e., pointing to our need for Him) or is the passage after Jesus' arrival (i.e., revealing Him as our only hope)?

The Bible is living and active.
It's very important to know that the Bible is unlike any other book in human history. It was written over a period of 1500 years, by more than 40 others, and yet it tells one unified story of redemption. Jesus told us, "The Holy Spirit would lead us into all truth." And it's the Holy Spirit that makes the Word of God alive and active in our life. Therefore the Bible is meant to be understood with the help of the Holy Spirit and is meant to be applied to our life.

The Bible is meant to be consumed, not just gone through.
When reading God's Word, I believe it's helpful to remember, quality over quantity. It's better to consume one verse that changes the way you see God or live your day than to read several chapters and not understand or apply any of it. As you read each day, pray a simple prayer asking God to give you a heart to receive His Word that day. You will be surprised at how God responds to that humble posture to receive real understanding.

01
DISCOVERY

The Word

Psalm 63, 2 Corinthians 4:1-16, Philippians 3:12-4:1

In Psalm 63, David declares that he is captivated by God's power and glory, and that God's "steadfast love is better than life." David said this as an older man, while on the run being betrayed by his own son, Absalom. The song of his life wasn't about the riches of his kingdom or the injustices he had faced in his life, but rather his song declared the inexhaustible glory and majesty of God. Positions, riches, and people could fail him, but he knew his "soul will be satisfied...when I meditate on you" (vs. 5-6).

Christianity and boredom can never be compatible. God is too awesome. Life is too short. The invitation is too great. The opportunities are too endless. Boredom is more a reflection of our lack of understanding than an accurate reflection of our circumstances. We have the opportunity in Christ, to walk with God—to live in relationship with Him daily. We have the opportunity to take risks because of His promptings. We have the opportunity to know Him through the revelation of His Word. Let's walk in this journey of true discovery. Let us "count everything else a loss compared to the surpassing worth of knowing Christ Jesus my Lord (Philippians 3:8)."

Prayer

"There is none like You, God! I worship You for who You are. Your steadfast love is better than life. I thank You for revealing Your beauty and glory to me. You are matchless and unending."

Obedience

Today, take time to meditate on God's majesty and beauty. How does this spark a desire to discover more of God?

02
RE-IMAGINE

The Word

Psalm 92, Ephesians 1:15-22, Ephesians 3:14-21, Colossians 1:9-23

The life of a follower of Jesus is full of the richness of Christ. His beauty, His matchless worth, His unending love are available to us every single day.

The word 'disciple' literally means a student or learner. When we say yes to Jesus' sufficiency to save us, we begin a lifetime of being a disciple as well. And so as a student of Christ, we set our vision on Jesus. He becomes our focus. He becomes our aim, our pursuit.

The prayer of Paul needs to be reinvigorated again in the heart of every Christ-follower. His prayer was that the "eyes of your heart may be enlightened (Ephesians 1:18)", that we may know the "immeasurable greatness of His power toward those who believe (Ephesians 1:19)", that we "may know the love of God which surpasses knowledge (Ephesians 3:19)," and that we "may be filled with the knowledge of His will in all spiritual wisdom and understanding (Colossians 1:9)." The great prayers of ever-increasing faith and knowledge to know God and walk with Him, are the prayers of people truly following as disciples.

Life is too short to settle for a religious sense of Christ that removes the joy, awe, and wonder from knowing Him. He purchased us with the highest price—His own life—to demonstrate the value of that which brings His Father glory. "And this is eternal life, that they might know you, the only true God, and Jesus Christ whom you've sent" (John 17:3).

Prayer

"I sit at Your feet today as a student. I want to know You more. I want to learn from You. Your ways are life to me."

Obedience

Today, take time to meditate on your identity as a disciple or student of Christ. How can Paul's apostolic prayers become personal for you and your vision of Christ?

03
DO YOU HAVE URGENCY?

The Word
Psalm 109, Ephesians 5:1-21, 1 John 4

Prayer is a conduit for the urgent. It's in the place of prayer that God aligns our hearts with things that are truly urgent. Then in prayer we can be activated for a life of true purpose and meaning.

In the kingdom, God calls us to live today for eternal purposes. The way of the kingdom is to be motivated by the values of this other kingdom (the kingdom of King Jesus) while living as foreigners in another land. Jesus introduced us to this way of life when He said, "the Kingdom of Heaven is at hand. (Matthew 4:17)" Or when He taught us to pray "on earth as it is in heaven (Matthew 6:10)." He began the era of "here but not yet." We live as citizens of another kingdom that is completely different from, and many times completely opposed to, the ways of the Kingdom of God. So our urgency for the wrong things can be stirred quite easily, without us even noticing it.

Our lives are short. Our opportunities are so great. The stakes only increase. The ripple effect only gets more pronounced. And eternity only gets closer. We need "look carefully then how you walk, not as unwise but as wise, making the best use of the time, because the days are evil" (Ephesians 5:15-16). We can live with an urgency that reflects the values of the Kingdom. We can love God wholeheartedly, love people sacrificially, and be obedient immediately.

Prayer

"Today, Lord, I uproot apathy. I instead pray for more urgency for eternal things. You are eternal and before all things, and today I pray for a glimpse of the things that move Your heart."

Obedience

Do you have urgency for things that matter? Or do you worry or get anxious about things that ultimately matter very little? How can you respond to God so that your heart aligns with His priorities?

04
DO YOU HEAR HIM KNOCKING?

The Word

Psalm 57, Revelation 2-3

Imagine Jesus sitting outside your house knocking on the front door. He wants to spend time with you. But He waits for you to let Him in. He is a gentleman. In Revelation 3:20, Jesus says to the church in Laodicea, "I stand at the door and knock. If anyone hears my voice and opens the door, I will come in to him and eat with him, and he with me." Why is it that some would not hear His voice? Or why is that some would hear His voice but not open the door. Why wouldn't we invite Jesus in?

In Revelation 3:14, Jesus is talking to the church in Laodicea. He is talking to people who are Christians or claim to be Christians. And the way He describes His current relationship with them is more as an uninvited guest. How did their relationship with Christ get to that point—that Jesus was viewed more as an intruding inconvenience than the central focus of life?

I often ask the question, is Jesus an outside guest in our churches or is He the Head of the church? Do we treat Him as an inconvenience or is He the honored King on the throne of our hearts? The promises for those who hear Him knocking, open the door and let Him in, are almost too amazing to wrap our minds around. And there is no middle ground. Jesus doesn't allow for a lukewarm middle ground. If we ignore Him, we are truly (spiritually speaking) poor, pitiable, blind, and naked. If we respond to Him and place Him centrally, He says we are rich, and clothed with beautiful garments. Every day we have the opportunity to open the door to King Jesus and let Him in fully to rule and reign in our hearts and lives. Let it be.

Prayer

"Today, Jesus I choose to open the door of my heart completely to You. I run from lukewarm Christianity and cling to the fullness that I read about. I know You are knocking on the door of my heart and I want to eagerly invite You to be the honored King of my life."

Obedience

Take time to repent of any apathy or complacency in your heart. Renew your commitment to invite Jesus in as honored King of your heart.

_____

_____

_____

_____

_____

_____

_____

_____

GOD CREATED US FOR *relationship* WITH HIM

truth 01

05
INTIMACY

The Word

Psalm 27, Psalm 42, Philippians 3:1-11

The greatest call upon a human life is to know God. It was God's desire so much that He gave His only Son so that it would be possible. Imagine if a person lived their entire life and never experienced the one thing they were created to experience more than anything else?

The gospel stands apart from all other religious messages because it states that we are sinful people before a holy God, and the way to forgiveness and redemption has been paved by Jesus' perfection, death, and resurrection. Every other religion is trying to make sense of the brokenness of this world and their solutions are the same. Their answer is to work harder on our side, to somehow clean ourselves up, to do certain good works, and hopefully achieve forgiveness before the gods. Unlike every other message, the gospel is good news because it's not about what we do, but what He did. It's a message about the work He did, not about the work we need to do to climb the mountain to God. It's that paradigm shift of the gospel that opens up the door to daily relationship and intimacy with God.

This paradigm shift is too intimidating for some They can accept the idea that a holy God could forgive them of their sins, but nothing more. In their minds, they get their ticket punched for heaven, their sins are absolved, but nothing more. For some, the idea of relationship with God seems irreverent. How can a holy, sovereign, all-powerful God have a relationship with obviously sinful, stubborn, finite human beings?

God has created you for relationship with Him. The greatest call upon your life is to know God personally, intimately, daily, and eternally.

Prayer

"I want to know You, Jesus. Thank You for making a way for me to come into friendship with God. Give me grace to respond to this central purpose of my life."

Obedience

Read Philippians 3:7-12 aloud. Submit everything else in your life to this greatest calling over your life to know God. Make this your prayer and take time to personalize this passage.

06
IDENTITY

The Word

Psalm 139, Romans 8, Galatians 3:23-4:7

A mentor in my life once told me, "Any time you sense insecurity in your life you have reached the extent of your understanding of the love of God." I've found this is true. Identity is a confidence in what God says about you. A lack of identity is a lack of security in your life. A life rooted in identity is built on a strong foundation. A lack of identity is subject to all of the whimsical labels, categories, or judgments of people in day-to-day life.

The Galatian church was being attacked by individuals who were trying to categorize or delegitimize them based on their background. The imposters were trying to exalt earthly status over kingdom status. The gospel re-writes the story of our lives. The gospel takes broken, rejected, bitter people and writes a new story. The gospel takes individuals from all walks of life, from "both sides of the railroad tracks", and from all ethnic groups and adopts them into a family. It truly is the most amazing story of all human existence.

Nobody other than you can jeopardize your position in Christ. We choose to be found in Him. We choose to abide and walk in the identity Christ purchased for us on the cross. We choose to grow in an increasing awareness of His Spirit's life inside of us. No circumstance, person, or crisis can affect that. The glorious gospel of Jesus Christ is the powerful story of redemption that transforms and makes new, if we will choose to walk in it. There is no more powerful narrative for our lives than the gospel. Paul said to the Colossians, "put on love...let the peace of Christ rule in your hearts...let the word of Christ dwell in you richly" (Colossians 3:14-16). If we want to experience the benefits of this new identity we have in Christ, we have to be active participants.

This is a lifelong call to be found complete and whole in Christ. We will make mistakes. We won't ever fully arrive, but there is a depth and richness to this message that will increase in profoundness as we live each day. Every day, in every changing season, in every shifting circumstance, we can discover the relevance of our identity in Christ.

Prayer

"Today, I choose to walk in my identity in You, Lord. I thank You for adopting me as Your own. Today I establish myself in You. Nothing else can have a hold on me. No other label or opinion from others means anything to me compared to what You think about me. I choose to walk fully in You."

Obedience

What labels or categories do you find yourself falling prey to (i.e., from society, family, or personal tendencies)? How often does your identity in Christ rule in your life? Meditate on the identity you have in Christ.

07
PURPOSE

The Word

Genesis 1, Psalm 23, Acts 17:22-34

Accidents are unfortunate. Sometimes accidents are completely unforeseen. Accidents are inconvenient. Accidents are inherently the dark side of probability. And therefore, I want to declare to you: you are not an accident!

Nothing in God's Word could give you the idea that you are an accident. This idea is given to us by the enemy. From the beginning, God created purposefully. He created all energy and matter—on purpose. He created all of the galaxies of the universe—on purpose. He specifically created the earth and our solar system—on purpose. He created water and all life—on purpose. When He created all of those things He said it was good (Genesis 1:25). And He created man, in His image, and positioned humanity above all living creatures, and after that He said, it was very good. With precision and purpose, He created you. With foresight and design, He destined you to walk in relationship with Him and live in the likeness of Him.

We are created for the glory of God. Our sense of purpose dictates the tone of our everyday lives. We can know how convinced we are of the purpose upon our lives by the way we use our time, resources, and talents. We can demonstrate our sense of purpose by the way we treat those closest to us or through the interactions we have with strangers. God doesn't create accidents. Instead, He "determined the allotted periods and boundaries of their dwelling place, that they should seek

God and perhaps feel their way towards him and find him" (Acts 17:26-27).

Prayer

"Creator God, thank You for creating me with a purpose. Help me, by Your grace, to live more and more aware of the purpose You have spoken over my life. I want to make the most of what You have given me. Help me Jesus!"

Obedience

Have you ever felt like an accident or an inconvenience to God or others? What does God's purposeful and designed story in Scripture say about your day-to-day life? What are some ways in which you could live with greater purpose?

GOD IS *not hard* TO FIND

02
truth

08
GOD IS FAITHFUL

The Word

Deuteronomy 7, 2 Chronicles 7:11-22, Psalm 26

Have you ever attempted to get a hold of someone repeatedly but without success? Maybe it's a friend that you have called, and texted, and even gone to their house, but you haven't received a single response. As I consider God's relationship towards us, it could easily be characterized in a similar way. God has consistently made Himself available to humanity. He has consistently revealed Who He is and what He is like, but often with no response.

God has revealed Himself time and time again. He has made Himself fully available, which as an infinite being will always be limited to finite beings. He has patiently and faithfully made Himself known. He has established a way for things to thrive and flourish, and when those ways are abandoned, catastrophe and destruction follows. The paths of obedience and disobedience are diverging paths. One way leads to life and one way leads to death.

Therefore, as we choose to respond to God, we respond with a posture of humility, brokenness, and repentance that recognizes that we are the ones who have been stubborn and unfaithful, and He is the One who has been waiting. He is faithful, while we are unfaithful. He is waiting, while we are rebellious. He had a plan of redemption for creation before creation existed, because that is Who He is. He is the faithful One. He is not hard to find because He knew us while we were in our mother's womb. He is not hard to find because at any moment we can choose to turn to Him and find Him there waiting, like a loving father.

Prayer

"Thank You for Your faithfulness, God. I realize that I am not faithful and yet You remain perfectly faithful. Today, I worship You for Your patient love toward me. Thank You for not giving up on me and thank you for giving me an opportunity to see You for Who You are."

Obedience

Take time to meditate on God's faithfulness. Thank Him for His unending faithfulness in your life.

09
RUNNING EVERYWHERE BUT GETTING NOWHERE

The Word
Psalm 51, Romans 1:16-32, Romans 5:1-10

I truly dislike running. Growing up playing sports, running was always a punishment. Running was the means to the end; it was never the end in itself. And to take it a step further, running on a treadmill was even worse. I just never understood it—running in place with nothing to show for it at the end of it all. If you like running, then I'm happy for you. You have found something to show for it, but I haven't.

The reality is, until we find Jesus, we are running everywhere but we get nowhere. It's like we are running in circles or running on a treadmill—exerting a lot of energy but accomplishing nothing, and ending up at the same place we started. A natural expression of our brokenness is our tendency to run to things other than God for comfort. We are all different in that regard. Some of us run to people to be our savior or assurance. Some of us run to pleasure and security in worldly pursuits. Sometimes we may run to the rush of losing ourselves in a hobby or interest. These things are cheap substitutes for God when we use them to fill a void they were never meant to fill.

We can have the world at our fingertips and yet feel empty without God. We can fill our lives with anything money can buy and still sense a void that only God can fill. It's important to recognize our innate need for God and our natural inclinations to fulfill that need. We all have a God-shaped hole in our hearts, and only God can fill it. At the heart of the gospel is God's extravagant expression of the reality that

He is making Himself available. He's always made Himself available to us, even when we've wanted nothing to do with Him. Jesus' life, death, resurrection, and sending of the Spirit, is God's radically generous gift declaring that you were created for Him. The problem has never been His availability, but rather on our willingness to run to Him.

Prayer is a way to run to the One who alone can fulfill us. We have the opportunity every day to run to God. We can stop running everywhere else and start solely running to Him. Prayer is our escape from the allure of our earthly lives. In prayer, we can run to God as our refuge.

Prayer

"Jesus, You are my everything. Nothing else fulfills or satisfies. You alone are my heart's desire. I want You to be the One I run to, time and time again. I choose to stop running to other things and I run to You."

Obedience

What is it you tend to run to other than God? Spend time today declaring to God your desire to run to Him and Him alone.

CALLING ON GOD DEMONSTRATES *dependence*

truth 03

10
GOD IS MY STRENGTH

The Word

Psalm 28, Ephesians 6:10-20

Prayer is an expression of trust. It is a demonstration of where we find our strength. When prayer moves from an obligation to a necessity, we know we have tapped into true prayer. God doesn't need prayer—we do. God doesn't need anything, but he gave us access to a conduit of conversation and relationship through His Son.

When a child falls and gets hurt, their natural response is to call out (or cry out). They are calling for help. They are hoping somebody who cares, and is able to help, will hear them and come to their rescue. In the Kingdom, we should never move beyond being a child of God. I'm not saying we should remain in immaturity or spiritual infancy, but we should never graduate from being a child of the Father. Greater maturity is greater dependency in the Kingdom. Greater dependency comes through a revelation of the source of one's strength. The key is to maintain a posture of calling on God that isn't just about the latest crisis, but is about a keen awareness of the constant need for Christ in our daily lives.

David said, "The Lord is my strength and shield; in Him my heart trusts, and I am helped. (Psalm 28:7)" Centuries ago, David was inspired by the Holy Spirit to demonstrate how to pray. He showed us we can call out to God as our strength and as our shield. The key now is to articulate a prayer of our own that communicates to God that He is our everything. We have been given a template, and now we can make it our own.

Prayer

"Today, Lord, I recognize that You are my strength. I want to grow to be more and more child-like in my dependence on You. Help me mature in the Kingdom by growing in complete dependence on you."

Obedience

Take time today to communicate to God that He is your strength. Take time to raise your voice and call out to God in dependence.

11
FRUITFUL

The Word

Psalm 37, John 15

All religions propose a form of prayer, but the gospel offers a different kind of prayer. It's a prayer in the form of depending on God. It's a mindset and consciousness of God. If prayer more closely resembles fretting, then we have it all wrong. As David says, "Fret not for yourself, it tends only to evil." And he also says, "Be still before the LORD and wait patiently for him" (Psalm 37:7-8). Prayer that frets is not useful prayer. Truly powerful prayer discovers the release of trusting God.

Fretful and fruitful are opposites. And fruitfulness in God's Kingdom comes from a place of resting or trusting in God. As Jesus describes it in John 15, it closely resembles us living like fruit-bearing branches connected to a vine. The fruitfulness comes out of our connection with the vine. Being fretful is a symptom of our lack of trust that He is able and can be trusted.

God really does care about every aspect of our life. There is not a single detail or thought that goes unseen to God. And therefore, fretting is a sign that we are clinging to control of our life. God can be trusted. When prayer shifts from spiritual fretting to active trusting, we will begin to experience fruitfulness in our lives.

Trusting God can be scary. Sometimes trusting God means something will be removed from our life. Sometimes trusting God means we need to be still and not do anything. And yet other times, trusting

God means jumping into immediate action. Trusting God doesn't always look the same but it always results in fruitfulness. Jesus gave us that promise in John 15:5 by saying, "Whoever abides in me and I in him, he it is that bears much fruit." Trusting God is fruitful, every time!

Prayer

"I choose to abide in You, Jesus. I recognize that apart from You, I can do nothing. I want my life to count and I want to bear fruit. So today, I choose being completely found in You. Thank you, Jesus!"

Obedience

Do what Psalm 37:7 says and be still before God. Take time to quiet yourself and your heart and meditate on the truth of who God is. "Delight yourself in the Lord and he will give you the desires of your heart" (37:4).

Jesus' name
IS THE WAY
TO THE
Father's
HEART

04
truth

YARD
WASTE
ONLY

12
IT'S NOT A FORMULA, IT'S THE GOSPEL

The Word
Psalm 20, John 14:1-14, John 17

It's Jesus Himself who teaches us to pray in His name. Praying in the name of Jesus is not a human tradition or invention. It is the faith-invoking catalyst to powerful prayer. Jesus prays, "Holy Father, keep them in your name, which you have given me, that they may be one, even as we are one" (John 17:11).

He is King Jesus. That is the name that will be written on the life of every one of His sons and daughters at the end of time (Revelation 3:12). His name points to the fullness of who He is and whose we are. King Jesus rules in this kingdom with all authority, honor, and perfection. Jesus was introducing this kingdom to a world that wanted nothing to do with it.

When we pray in the name of Jesus, we are verbally aligning our own lives as His kids, and position as subjects to King Jesus. Praying in the name of Jesus is a constant reminder of the essence of the kingdom—it's Jesus. We pray in His name because it's only through His perfect sufficient sacrifice that we can come before the Father. We pray in His name because He demonstrated His authority over sin, death, and the enemy. We pray in His name because we are His children, bought with a high price. We pray in His name because we are participants in His kingdom and we do His work.

Prayer

"Lord Jesus, today I thank You for equipping me with authority to pray in Your name. I do not pray in my own strength or authority. Instead, I stand with authority in Your name as a child—called and appointed. Thank you!"

Obedience

Name two other areas of life where authority is granted in someone's name (i.e., government, law enforcement, politics). Center your faith on the authority Jesus grants you to pray in His name. Take time to specifically pray in His name.

_____

_____

_____

_____

_____

_____

_____

_____

_____

13
SONS, DAUGHTERS, AND HEIRS

The Word

Psalm 8, Luke 15:11-32, John 14:15-3, Ephesians 1:1-14

My wife, Tanya, and I have four kids. Each of them are our kids. We never doubt that fact; we were there when they were born and we know they are our children. They never doubt it either. We are all they have ever known. But what if they woke up one day and didn't believe they were really our kids? What if they doubted that most basic truth about where they belong?

In the gospel story, it's a little different. We are born into this world as orphans, like sheep without a shepherd. We didn't belong anywhere—outside of Christ we are wanderers. But when we encounter Jesus, that all changes. Through His perfect Son, we hear the voice of the Father calling us home. He calls us to be adopted into His family, to be called children of God. And we pray and operate from that place of adoption.

When we pray in the name of Jesus, we are invoking faith initiated through grace, to remind our hearts that we are not orphans, but chosen sons and daughters. Jesus tells the story of the lost son in Luke 15 and when he welcomes the younger son home, he says "put a ring on his hand" (vs. 22). Even though the son didn't deserve it, the father gave him a signet ring. This was a family signet ring given to each member with the right to do business in the name of the family. As sons and daughters in God's family, we go about doing His work in His name and never doubting it for a moment.

When we pray as children of God, we are praying as co-workers and heirs to His kingdom. We are not outsiders hoping for the best. We are not trying to twist the arm of a far-off God. No, instead we belong and are called to do business in the kingdom—to be about the Father's work. When we don't pray, we are neglecting the priorities of God.

Our prayers often reflect our forgetfulness. We sometimes pray as outsiders. We have a direct way to the Father's heart—our Father's heart—because of the perfect way created by Jesus. We have been adopted, chosen, and we belong.

Prayer

"I call out to my Father and I know You hear me. You have picked me and adopted me as Your own. Now I belong. Now You have granted me a place in Your family. You have called me to share Your priorities. Give me grace to walk today with a convincing sense of belonging in my adopted family."

Obedience

Take time to boldly pray to the Father. Spend time thanking Him for choosing you and adopting you into His family.

PRAYER IS OUR PLACE OF *authority* AS BELIEVERS

truth 05

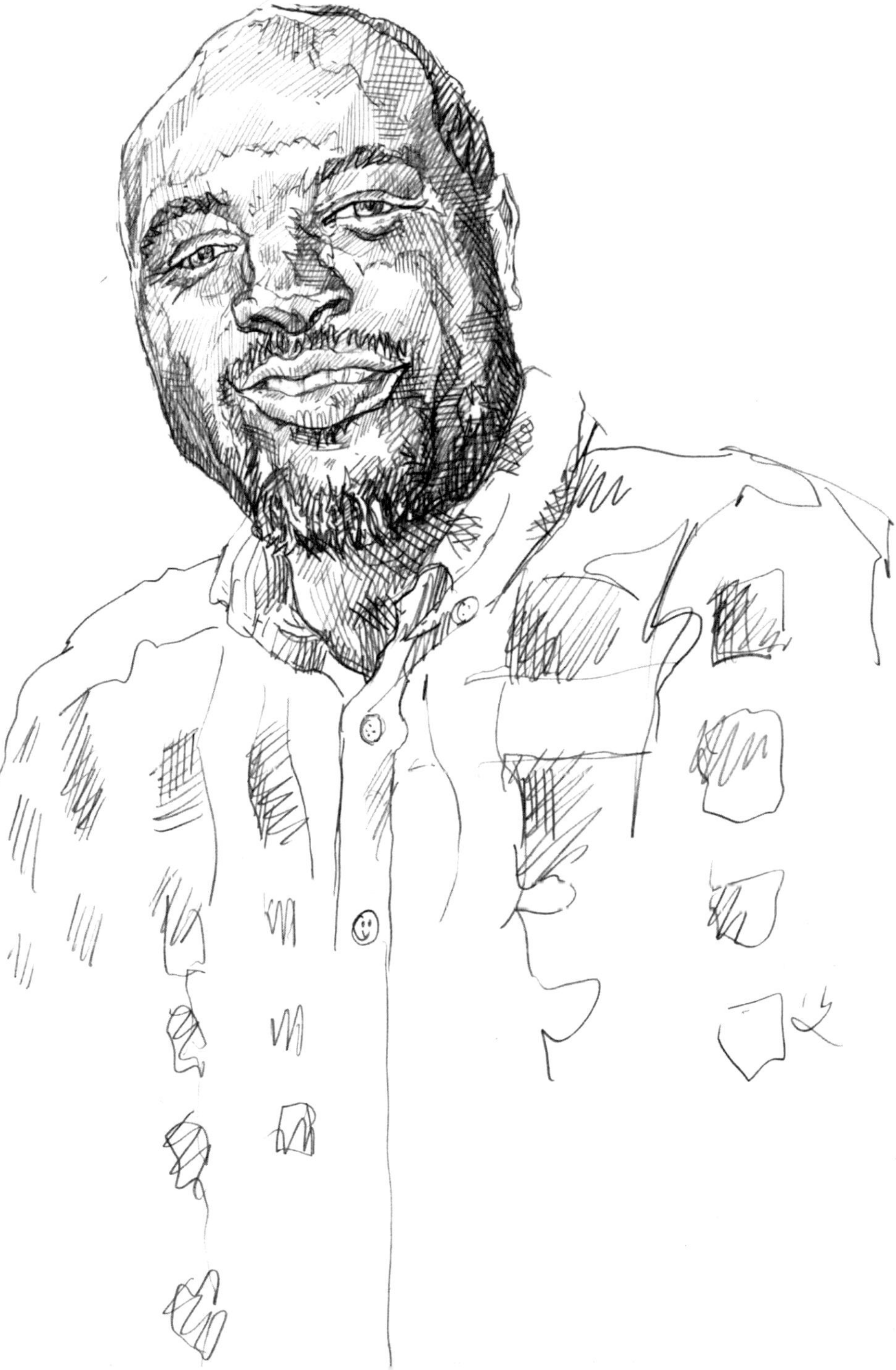

14
THE GOSPEL OF GRACE

The Word
Psalm 25, Galatians 4:1-7, Hebrews 4

What do we do with the message of grace? It seems too good to be true. It seems too generous. It can be difficult to receive the grace poured out on us through Jesus. Jesus' grace calls us to come confidently before the throne of God. We can know that there is mercy available as we approach the throne of God. We can know that the chasm of separation between us and God was massive, and yet Jesus willingly bridged it. Each of us are familiar with our own hearts and know the sinful nature that still rears up in our lives. How does the grace of God call us to confidently draw near?

In the Old Covenant, a lot went into a priest entering the Most Holy Place within the tabernacle or the temple. The rites required burning incense, ceremonial washings, and a sacrifice on behalf of the people and the priest. The priest had to wear the proper attire and follow the commands precisely. This was a matter of life and death. There are accounts in the Old Testament of people dropping dead because of the slightest misstep in light of the holiness of God (1 Samuel 6:19, 2 Samuel 6:2-7). This should convince us of God's perfect holiness, and that what Jesus did was no small thing.

Jesus' sacrifice is the bold declaration to humanity of the power of His forgiveness and love. He can make a way for enemies to be brought near as friends. He makes it possible for broken people to stand before Him redeemed, washed clean, and as children of God. When we see Jesus in His authority, boldly making a way for each of us, we realize the reciprocation needed to be bold in return. We can draw near with confidence because we know that Jesus' way is the perfect way and the only way.

We experience authority as a believer when God convinces us we are not an accident. In the throne room of grace, everyone is powerfully equipped to experience a breakthrough with God.

Prayer

"Jesus, I thank You that Your grace made a way for me. There was nothing I could do to make things right. But You did it. You made a way when there was no way. You are my Father and I know You hear my prayer."

Obedience

In Galatians 4, Paul says our spirit cries out "Abba, Father". Abba is an Aramaic informal term for father. Call out to God as your Dad or Father. Today, pray confidently to your Father about the things on your heart. Approach Him with boldness through the grace of Jesus.

15
AUTHORITY IN CHRIST

The Word
Psalm 3, Matthew 28:16-20, Mark 16:14-19, Luke 24:36-49

Prayer is not a 'shot in the dark.' It's not a whimsical attempt or last resort. We are commissioned by Jesus to live lives of faith in a relationship with Him. Jesus said, "ALL authority in heaven and earth has been given" to him (Matt. 28:18). And it was in that place of ultimate authority that He commissioned His rag-tag group of followers to go and turn the world upside-down.

Many times, I have heard individuals talk about their lack of confidence when it comes to prayer. Or I have heard people say that they tried praying and it didn't work. Or I have realized that what some =call prayer is really just worrying out loud. Wherever we land in those different misconceptions about prayer, rest assured that God has something far better for us in prayer.

Imagine you are in a big room filled with people. The room is loud and many conversations are taking place all around. But then, seemingly out of nowhere, one person catches your attention and that person calls you over. You make your way across the room and come before him and you begin to talk to him. He looks at you blankly, and then looks confused. You attempt to explain what you saw from across the room, when he called you over (or so you thought). The conversation ends abruptly because obviously what you thought was the beginning of a great connection was nothing more than an awkward social mistake and he must have been calling for someone else.

This scenario is very similar to how we often treat prayer. We say theologically that God called us into relationship with Him. But then somehow prayer becomes nothing more than a timid attempt to merely touch base with God. What Jesus has made available to us is prayer with authority. We can know that He called us from across the room and the conversation He is calling us into is not a mistake or an awkward moment for Him. When we come before Him, He sighs and says, 'This is what I have destined. This is what I have been calling you to.' He's not caught off guard by it, surprised by it, and there is no mistaking God's cues.

He has really called you into a conversation. There's no mistaking that. We enter that conversation with God through prayer because of the authority of Jesus. There is a commissioning authority that we can sense upon our lives when we run into the place of prayer.

Prayer

"I know You called me, Jesus. And I choose to respond to You. You have left no doubt about Your love for me. And in response I choose to flesh out this relationship with You. I want to live in greater and greater intimacy with You."

Obedience

Take time to meditate on the truth that the Father gave His Son all authority on heaven and earth, and Jesus commissions us from that place of authority. Take time to worship Him for calling you by name with a purpose and commissioning you. Allow that authority to usher you into a time of powerful prayer about the things on your heart.

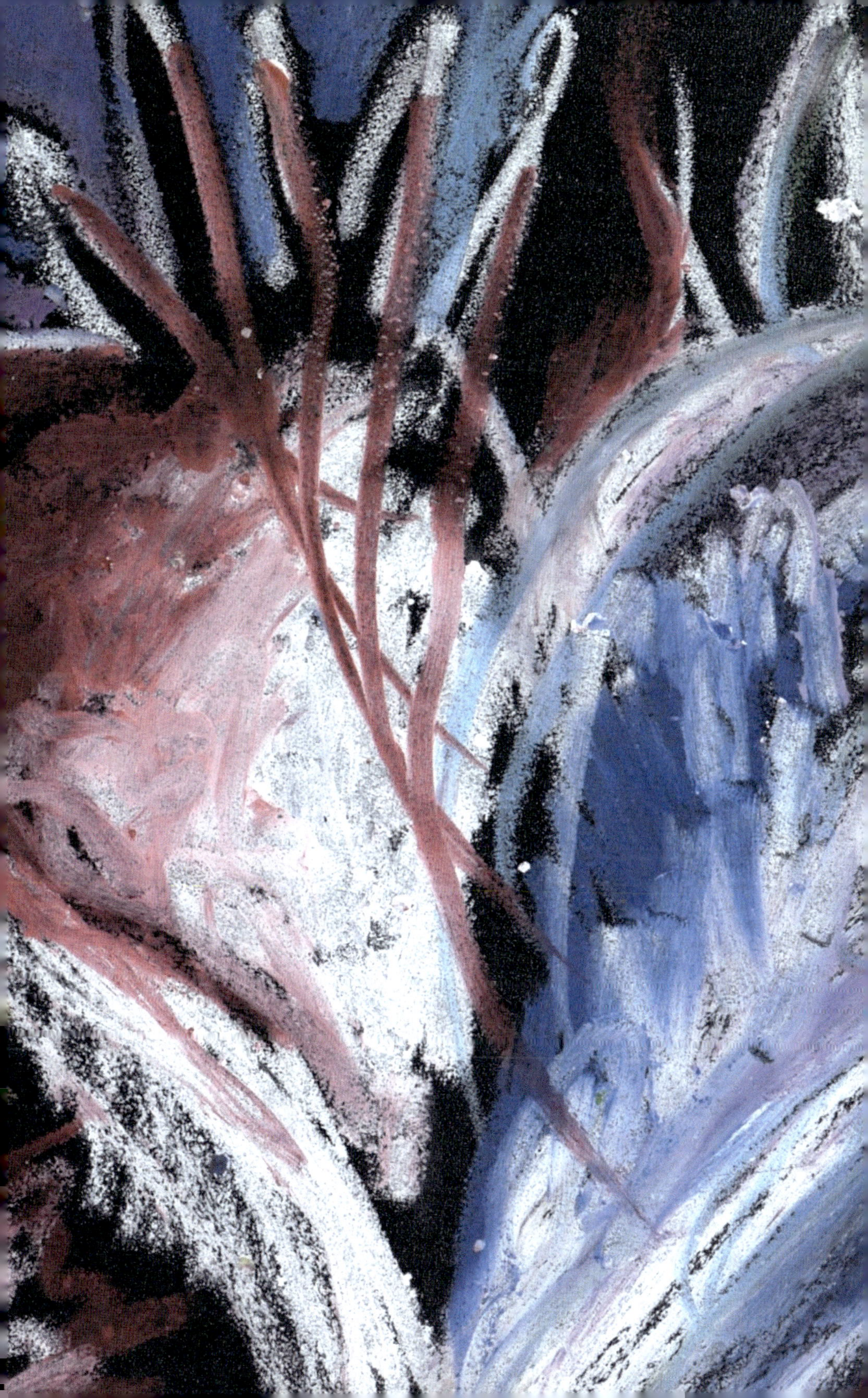

FAITH RESTS IN WHAT WE KNOW ABOUT *God's character* AND *His promises*

truth 06

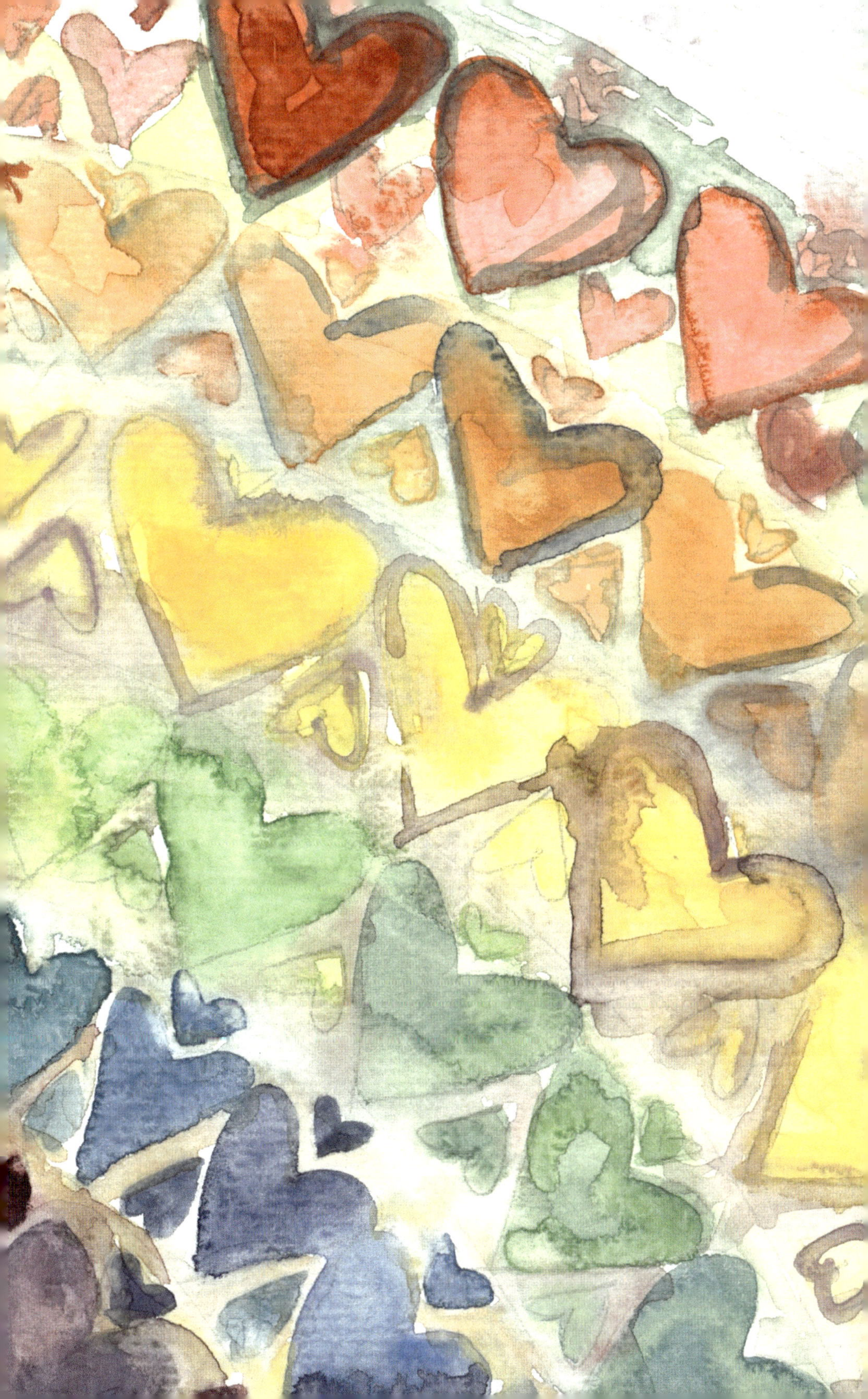

16
KEEPING PROMISES

The Word

Psalm 89, Hebrews 10, 2 Peter 3

Last summer, I promised to take my 7-year-old daughter on a father-daughter date. I had told her several days prior, and asked her to let me know what she wanted to do for this special afternoon out. Her top pick was to go to a little snow-cone shack down the road from our house. Unfortunately, I spoke too soon and too confidently and said, "Let's go for it. We are going to go eat snow-cones for our date."

The little roadside snow-cone shack had a reputation for having inconsistent hours, so I planned to take her on a weekend and I looked up their posted hours online before we left the house. We drove the couple blocks down the street and I saw darkness in the windows and a fateful sign out front. Closed. On top of that, it wasn't just closed for the day, it was closed and for sale. The whole thing was going out of business. My confident words of assurance were sorely disappointed by real life. There was no way we could enjoy snow-cones together that day. It just wasn't going to happen. Hopes were dashed and my child got a lesson in disappointment.

The Kingdom of God gives us a lesson in learning to trust again. We have to learn to take God at His word. When God gives a promise, it cannot be broken. We can mess it up, but He can't. We have to learn to uproot cynicism and become like a child again, this time as a child of God in the kingdom of heaven. God's story of redemption is full of promises. His promises have sustained His children for centuries. And it's no different today—God has given us His promises to propel us forward, fixating on truth and His character.

This doesn't mean our lives always go the way we planned (any heroes of the faith from the Bible can attest to that), but it does mean God's promises will stand true and untouched. We deal with disappointment in life by bringing it to the Father, not by letting it distance us from the Father. When we learn to bring our real frustrations, discouragements, and disappointments to the Father we recognize His work in our lives, and our vision for what really matters gets honed and refined. We get disappointed only when our expectations and plans diverge from God's plan for our lives.

For a list of God's promises that are relevant to us today in the New Covenant, check out the Appendix in the back of this book.

Prayer

"I want to trust You, God. I know I have been rejected and people have failed me, but I choose to fully open my heart to You. I don't want to hold back anymore. I choose to renew my mind in Your promises and who You have revealed Yourself to be."

Obedience

Take time today to voice any cynicism, unbelief, or disappointment to the Lord. He's not caught off guard by it and He is more than able to help you as a child of God towards faith in his promises. Try to see where your disappointments were the result of unrealistic expectations or straying from God's plan for your life. Then take time to speak out the promises of God (provided in the Appendix).

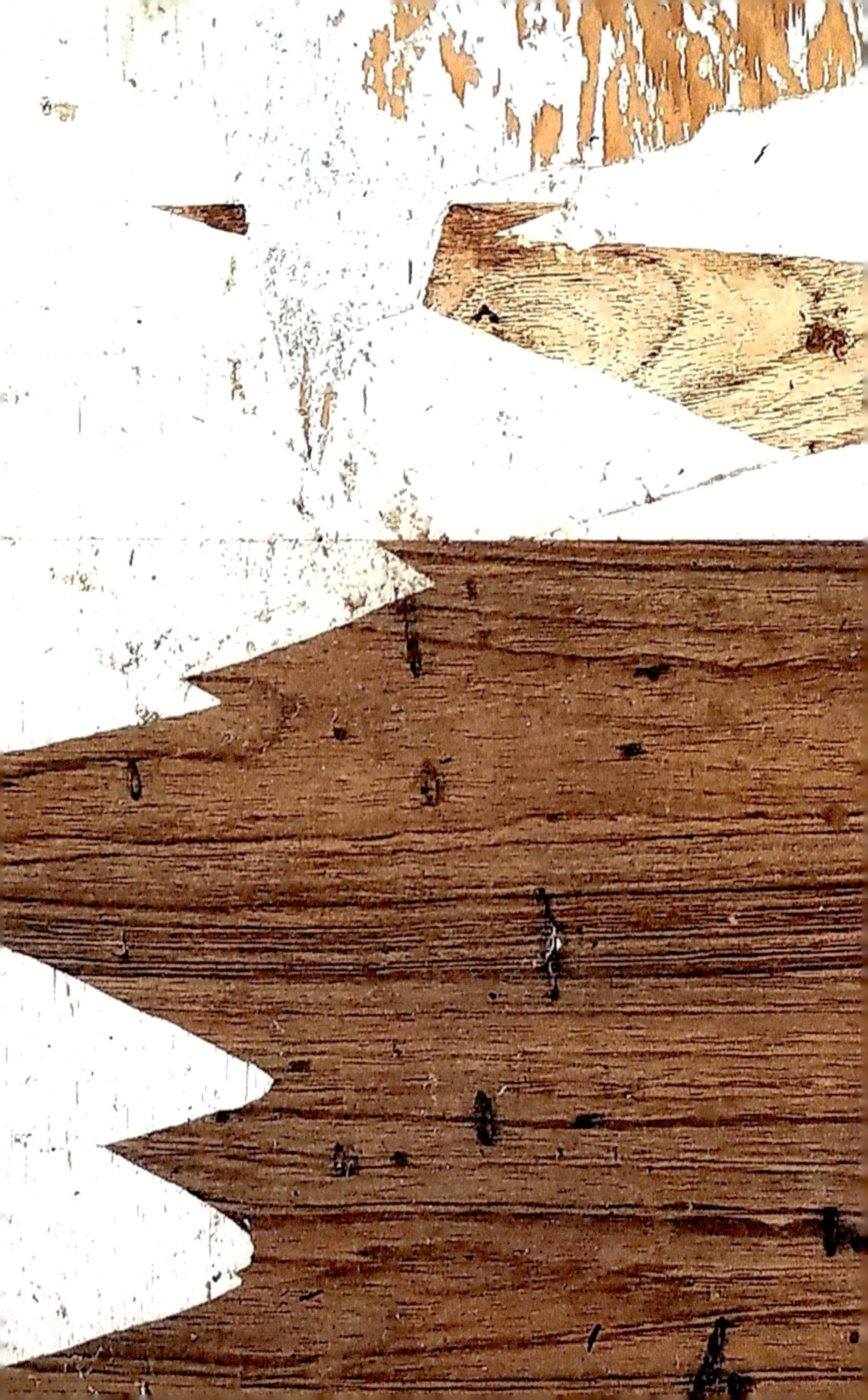

17
GENUINE FAITH THROUGH A RENEWED MIND

The Word

Psalm 1, Romans 12, 1 Peter 1:13-25

I remember the adrenaline rush of cramming right before a big exam in college. That's common. There's a sense of anticipation to get through the immediate pressure point of an intense class. And then there is a rush of feel-goods that hits you when you make out on the other side with a good grade. It's like a sigh of relief and a boost of confidence. But we all know deep down, even in academics, that this type of preparation is not ideal. The purpose of learning is not to to pass exams—the purpose is to absorb the information and gain a level of competent understanding that can be applied.

How often do we treat the Word of God like material for a big exam? It can easily be reduced down to the bare minimum to get us through the season of testing or growth that we find ourselves in. Or we binge on the Word in times of desperation, when we know we need to 'pass the test.' But when we do that, we are missing the point.

God's Word, when properly applied in our lives, becomes a recalibration tool. God draws us back to Himself, His will, and His plans in our lives. His Word is not as useful when it comes to just passing the test before us. His Word is meant to be consumed and understood on a deeper level that impacts the way we see God, the world around us, and ourselves.

And so, finally, when we allow the Word of God to pour over us, slowly, consistently, convincing us of God's perfect ways, it begins to impact the way we pray. Our prayer begins to more genuinely reflect a pure conversation between a child and his/her perfect Dad. Our prayers begin to boldly ask and seek for the things we know are the desires of God's heart. Prayer then begins to be a natural expression of our heart's understanding, and we say goodbye to the days of floating from test to test.

Prayer

"God open up Your Word to me in new ways. I want the Word to be the steady diet that fuels my prayer life. Give me a heart that understands Your Word and grace to apply it to my everyday life. Help me, Jesus!"

Obedience

Pray Romans 12:1-2 over yourself. Make a commitment to God that you fully surrender yourself to His truth. Pray for God to transform you through the renewing of your mind. Over the days to come, take time to reflect on how God's truth impacts your prayer life.

GOD REWARDS
persistence

truth 07

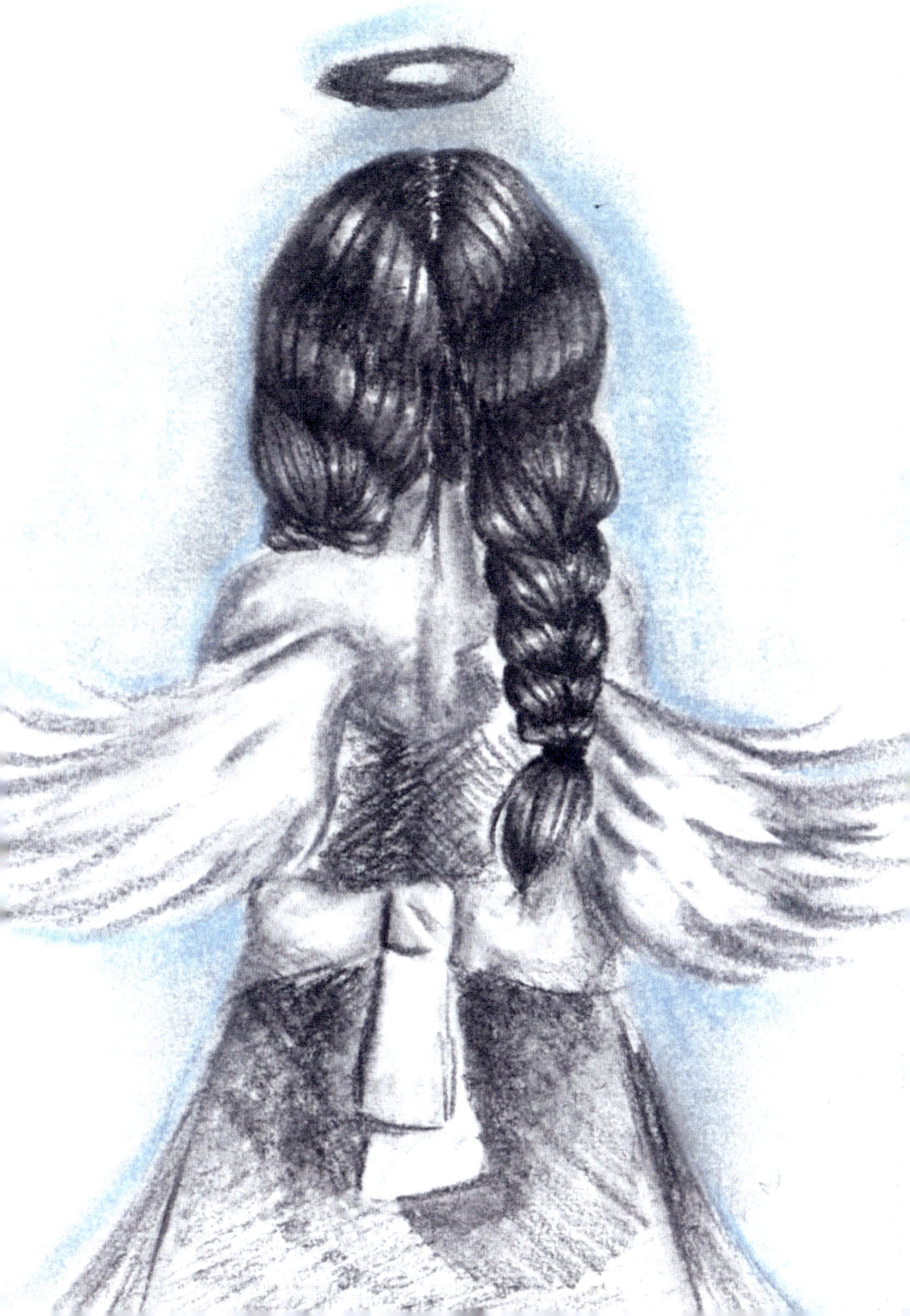

18
THE MYSTERY OF THE KINGDOM

The Word

Psalm 13, Daniel 10, Luke 18:1-8

It is good to embrace mystery. Mystery is not bad. Mystery keeps us humble and child-like. Mystery keeps us dependent. And I would say, it's good and healthy to declare out loud certain mysteries that exist in the kingdom of God. One of those mysteries is the reality that God rewards persistence.

There is a real tension before us. On one side, God gives us many great and precious promises, and a robust picture of His redemptive story (past, present, and future). But on the other side, we never seem to know God's timing, or exactly how it will play out. When you think back through the stories of redemptive history, Noah didn't know when the rains were coming, Abraham didn't know when his son would be born, David didn't know when his kingship would be realized, Isaiah didn't know when the Messiah would be welcomed, the first believers didn't know when the Holy Spirit would be poured out, and the list could go on and on. In fact, it's hard to think of a single instance when a promise is linked to a specific timing of its fulfillment.

There is a principle being demonstrated and Jesus emphasizes it in Luke 18, that God rewards the persistent. There is fruit when we press in and persevere through the unknowns. I think for many, this kingdom reality is difficult to accept. And on one hand, it feels like blind faith. But it's not blind faith. In reality, God has given us countless examples of the way He works in our lives, and every time He reveals a promise, but not the timing. And even more than that, He lays out this kingdom principle explicitly, "he told them a parable to the effect that they ought always pray and not lose heart" (Luke 18:1). The promises are clear, but the timing is not. We don't always need to know the "why" of God's timing. Of course, we can think of the character that God wants to develop in us or the grandeur of His plan, but those answers just help ease our minds. At the end of the day, we don't know why the timing is mysterious. We just know we are invited to be active participants in a kingdom full of promises. And the world needs followers of Jesus more enthralled by faith in God and His promises than overwhelmed by disappointment or disillusionment. God rewards persistence.

Prayer

"I trust Your timing, God. Give me grace to be one who is called persistent. I trust that Your promises are for me and that You will reward me for persevering."

Obedience

Write out two or three things you have been praying for or hoping for change. Give them to the Lord in a fresh way knowing that He rewards persistence.

_____

_____

_____

_____

19
THINGS WORTH FIGHTING FOR

The Word
Psalm 86, Mark 9:14-29, 1 Corinthians 9:19-27, 2 Timothy 2:1-13

I played sports in high school and back then it seemed intense. It wasn't because we were the biggest and best school around for sports, but because most of us loved the sport. And what's the point of playing if you're not going to give it your all? I remember practicing twice a day in the heat of summer for football, or strength training for basketball or track. It seemed like there was always something more you could be doing to get better and be better than your opponent. It seemed like we could work hours per day and push each other intensely because the result would be worth it.

Paul gives a similar example in 1 Corinthians 9 regarding our spiritual lives when he says, "we do it to receive an imperishable prize" (vs. 25). We do what? He says we run the race to win; we exercise self-control like an athlete for a higher purpose. In the light of eternity, the earthly things we concern ourselves with pale in comparison to things that really matter. Politics, sports, our possessions. All of those things can drive us to do some crazy things, to be made a fool, or to surrender a lot. But what about things of eternal significance?

I think the church is seen as irrelevant to the world because the church rarely burns for things that matter. The world should see a church burning white-hot for eternal things. But all too often, the church wallows in irrelevance because we are bored in our Christianity and more fascinated by our buildings and programs, than any sort of relevant power. What if we began to contend for things that actually mattered? That is the church that really makes a difference. The lost, the brevity of this life, the ruling ethic of love, the supernatural power of God, these are all eternal matters that should compel the church forward with a tenacity and intensity that is completely uncommon. These things should compel us to passionate prayer—like Jesus prayed. He prayed out of necessity in light of the eternal realities before Him. He didn't pray because of religious obligation, or social pressure, or to soothe His conscience. Instead, He prayed because He needed to hear the heart of the Father for the moment.

What if the church had that sort of persistence in her contending? What if the church felt that conviction of the importance of this holy moment, and knew God was the only hope? What if?

Prayer

"O Lord, give me a heart that burns for things that truly matter. Help me turn from things that are worldly. I don't want them anymore. I want to be compelled with a passion for things that will matter in the light of eternity."

Obedience

Take time to repent of any apathy in your prayer life. Ask God to light a fire in your heart for the things that really matter. Pray that God would break your heart and speak to you about the things that have eternal significance.

_____

_____

_____

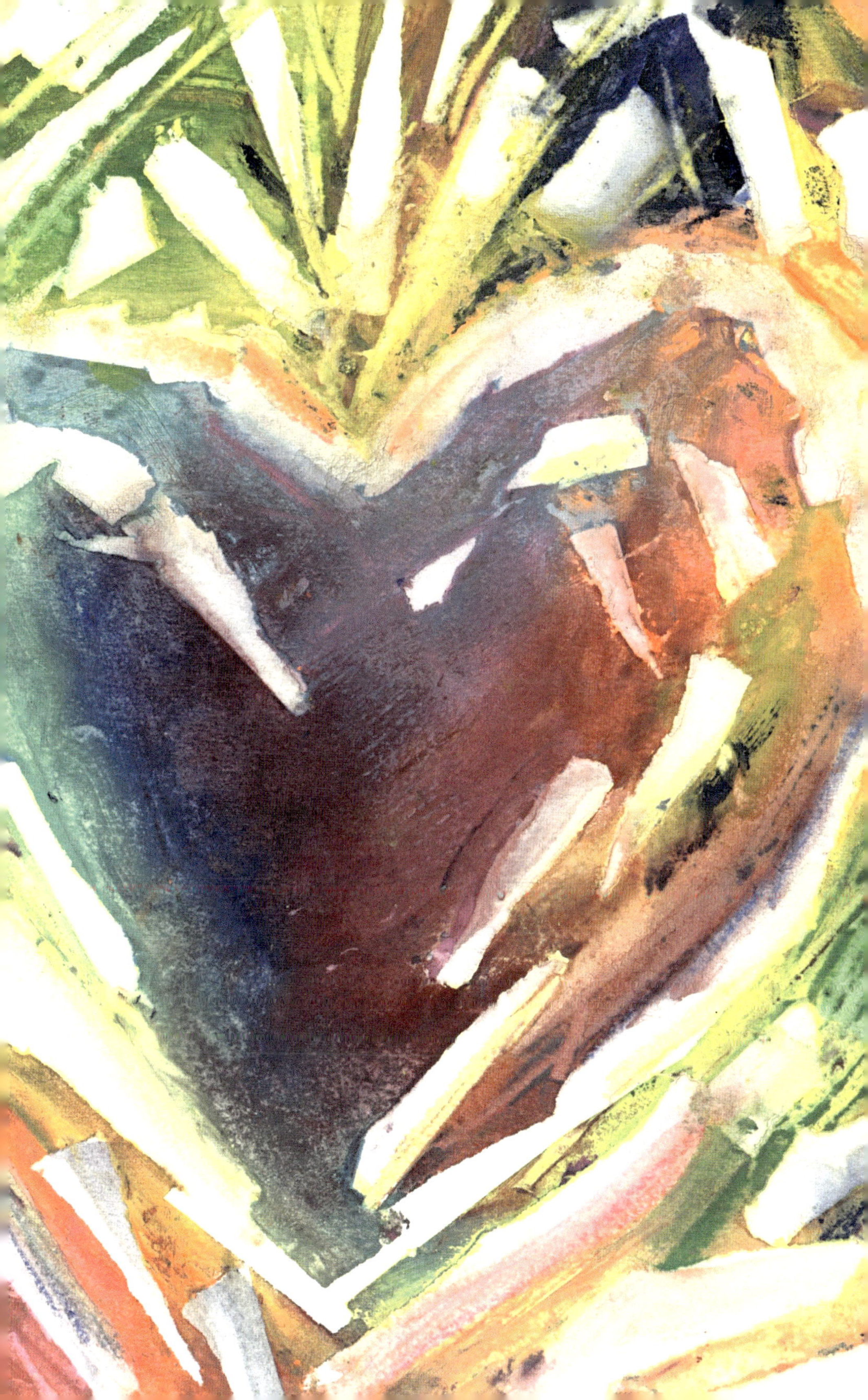

GOD USES *desperate* PEOPLE

08

truth

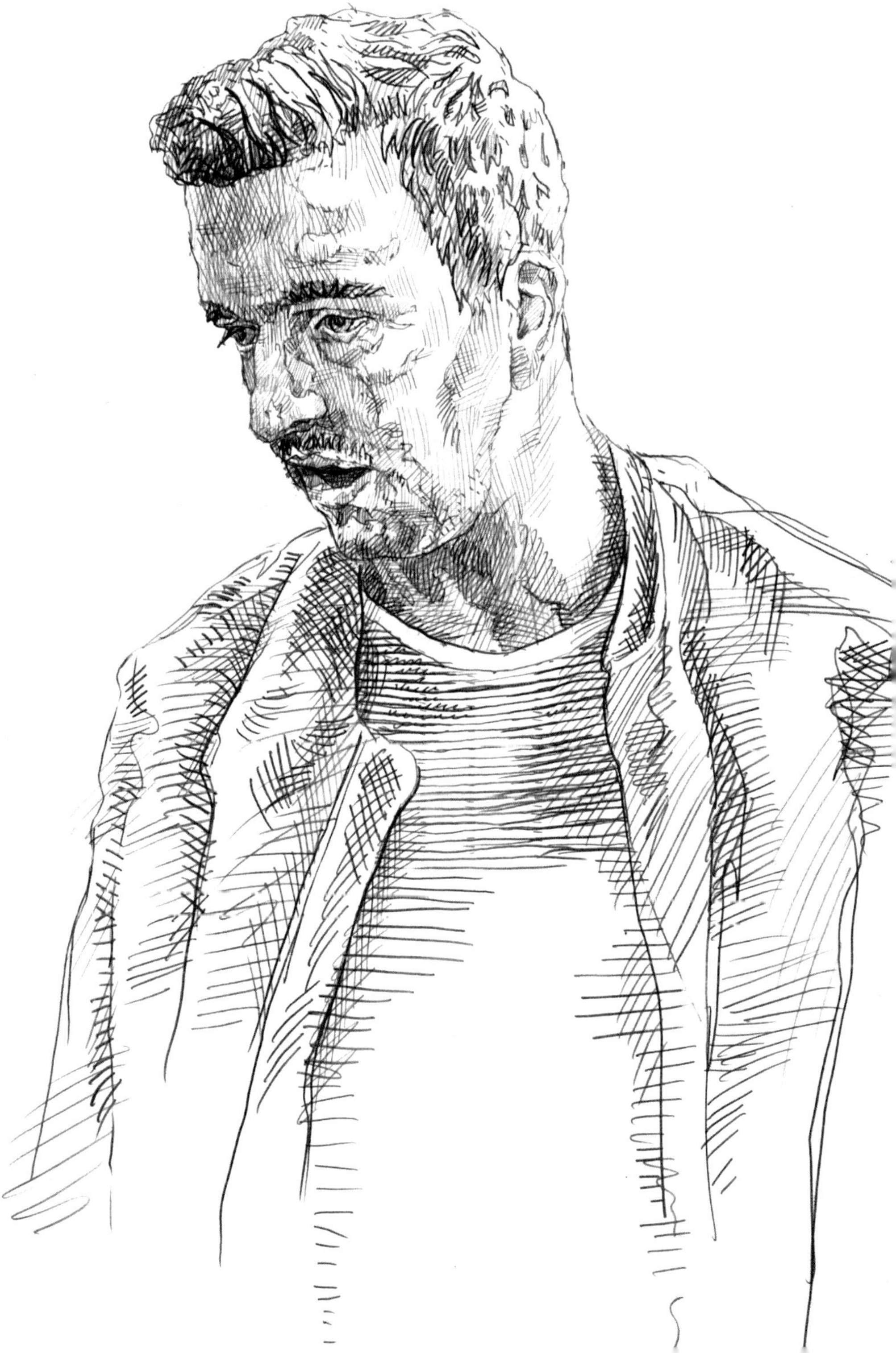

20
EMBRACE DESPERATION

The Word

Psalm 143, Matthew 5:6, Mark 2:1-11

"I tell you the truth, unless a kernel of wheat is planted in the soil and dies, it remains alone. But its death will produce many new kernels—a plentiful harvest of new lives" (John 12:24).

God draws beauty out of struggle. Desperation is the refining fire that purifies our hopes and motivations. Our faith is drawn to new heights through that pure hunger and desperate desire.

Everyone needs to come to an end of themselves—where self-reliance ends and God-dependence starts. Harvest comes out of death (John 12:24). Blessing comes out of hunger and thirst (Matthew 5:6). Reward comes out of sacrifice. If you lose your life, you will find it. As a hard-working perfectionist, it was tough for me to discover this. I can fall prey to the lie that that there is something more I can do to fix my situation or get us out of a difficulty. But so much of life is out of our control. And when it comes to the most meaningful things in life, God is our only hope.

God wants to root out our self-reliance and longing for control. It exists in every one of us and when we learn to embrace desperation, we begin to let go of all that. We learn to lean into God and depend on Him.

Prayer

"Today, I confess my desperate need for You. I want to give up trying to control everything in my life. I realize I need You. You are my only hope!"

Obedience

Take time today to express your desperate dependence on God. Whatever significant pressures you are carrying, cry out to God as though everything depends on Him, because it does.

21
A HISTORY OF DESPERATION

The Word

Psalm 16, Jeremiah 17:1-18, Daniel 9:1-23, Mark 7:24-30

God has always used desperate people. The desperate ones are now heroes of the faith. The desperate ones were those who allowed their impossible situation to push them towards God. And we, today in the 21st century, are blessed to look back over history and be emboldened by these desperate ones who went before us. Their lives are a testimony that inspires us with truth.

During possibly some of the darkest years of Israel's history, the prophet Daniel was desperate. He faced overt attacks on his faith and was surrounded by a culture of idol worship and false gods. The only reports he heard from his homeland were of desolation and destruction. It didn't seem like it could get much worse. But Daniel refused to be victimized. He refused to allow his situation to dictate his faith. He became a desperate man.

If we aren't careful, our complacency can fool us into thinking the broken situations around us are normal. Rather than allowing these obstacles to push us to desperation, we settle for the status quo. I believe many of the most desperate people are rejected by their own generation, because what they see as worth contending for is so radical that it's rejected by the mainstream. Most prophets in the Bible were seen as crazy people by their contemporaries. They caught a glimpse of God's heart for a city, a nation, a people, and they refused to be denied.

Daniel prayed, "O my God, incline your ear and hear...Pay attention and act. Delay not, for your own sake, O my God, because your city and your people are called by your name" (Daniel 9:18-19). This is the prayer of a desperate man in the midst of a desperate situation. May we press in and allow the desperate people to inspire us a fresh.

Prayer

"God thank You for giving me a treasure trove full of biblical examples of those who desperately pressed in with faith. I pray their examples would fuel my prayer life, to contend with faith and passion, knowing that You use the most desperate people."

Obedience

Try to put yourself in Daniel's position—spiritually isolated, surrounded by spiritual darkness, seemingly far removed from God's promises for His people. Daniel saw something different. Take time today to allow your heart to burn with desperation for transformation, revival, and change in the situations and people around you.

breakthrough
IS OURS
IN JESUS

09 truth

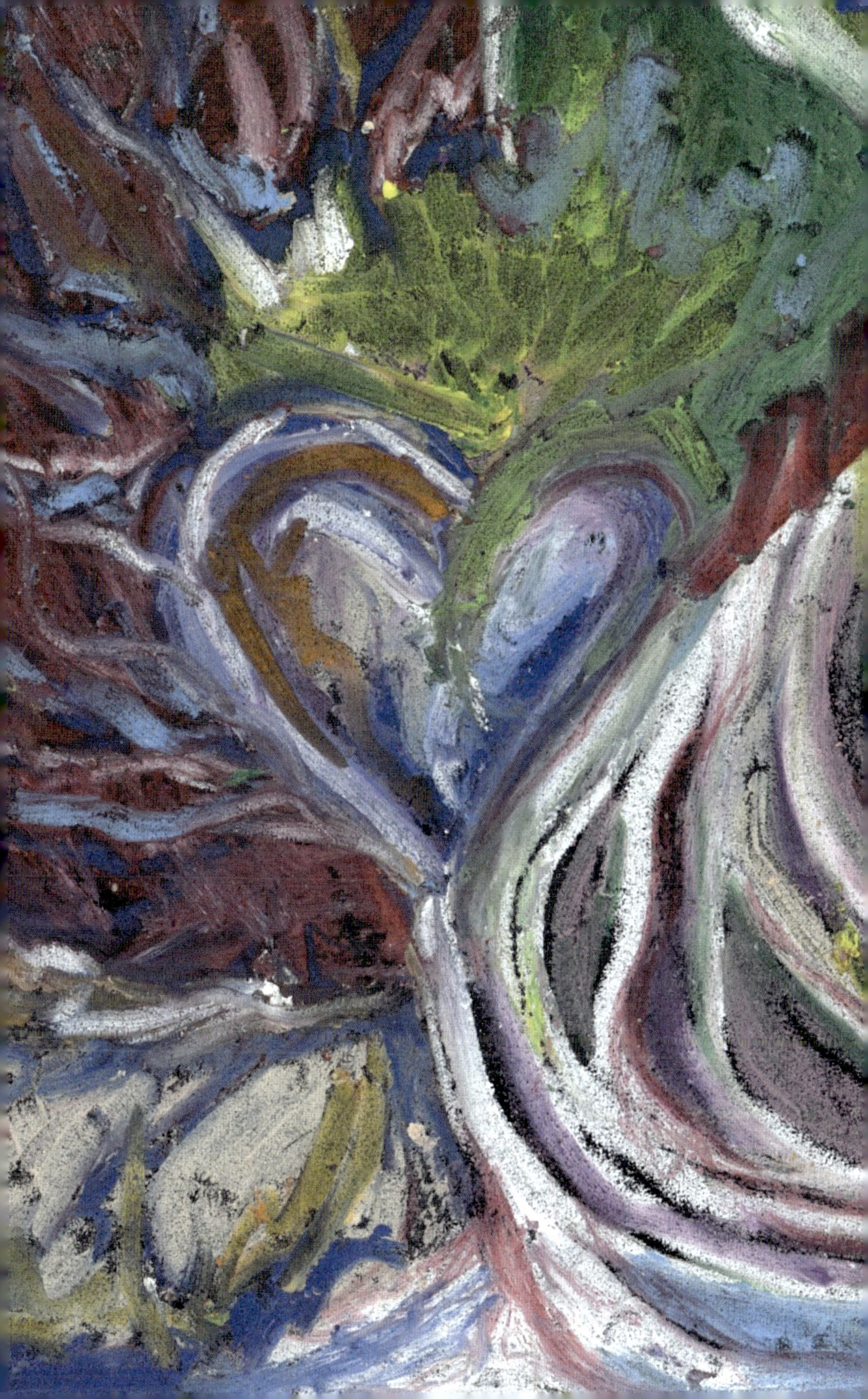

22
READ IT AND BELIEVE IT

The Word

Psalm 111, Matthew 7:7-11, 2 Corinthians 10:1-6

Too often we allow our experiences to form our theology. We experience a lack of miracles, or certain disappointments, or unanswered prayers, and we conclude that God must have changed. We assume that our experiences are a better commentary on life than God's Word.

The chasm between our experiences and God's promises is an invitation into prayer. I believe God is raising up a new generation of praying people that take God at His Word and truly contend for breakthroughs we are promised. This requires a change in our mindset.

We are often told that we need "to see it to believe it". This naturalistic mindset concludes that things only matter if they are measurable and tangible. But, in Jesus, we are ushered into a new paradigm of living, almost caught between two worlds. The Kingdom is here, but not yet. The challenge then becomes for us to live more compelled by what we know to be true in the Kingdom of God than what seems to be true in the kingdom of this world around us. We need to transition to a mindset of looking into God's Word and believing what it says.

We need to read it and believe it. And when we believe the promises are ours, then we make a decision to be people of breakthrough. The Kingdom of God needs people that are willing to stand in the gap and push in, knowing that breakthrough only comes when people humble themselves and contend for God's purposes.

Prayer

"Jesus, I choose to believe the testimony of Your Word. I choose to submit my experiences to the lens of Your Word. Anything that doesn't line up pushes me to seek You in faith, believing for the breakthrough."

Obedience

Take time today to confess to God ways in which your experiences have impacted your theology. Maybe it was a disappointment, an unanswered prayer, a tragedy. Confess those to God and then spend time asking Him to re-form your beliefs on the truth of His Word.

23
THE STAKES ARE HIGH

The Word
1 Kings 18:20-46, Nehemiah 1, Psalm 84

Ultimately God will accomplish what He wants. But God has chosen to use people like you and me to bring about His redemptive plan. He chooses to use regular, broken people to be part of His beautiful story of restoration.

So when it comes to our inaction, or lack of prayer, much is at stake. We can play a part in what God wants to do. Or God can use someone else. I desire to be on the frontlines. I desire to make my life count. I desire to take bold stands that significantly shake up the status quo.

James tells us that Elijah was just a normal guy like you and me, but he often chose not to do what was normal. He chose to stand up against the hundreds of prophets of Baal. He chose to trust God for food and water during a drought. He chose to pray for rain when the land desperately needed rain. He was continually willing to be the one who stood in the gap, the one who took the risk and made it count.

Today is a fresh opportunity. There are injustices all around us that God has given us answers for. There are cycles of brokenness that God wants to bring to an end. There are people who are discouraged and hopeless that God wants to encourage. But the reality is, He uses normal people like you and me. Let's recognize what's at stake and make the most of today.

Prayer

"Lord, thank You for today. Help me, today, to recognize the opportunities. I want to make a difference. I want my life to count. I choose to take risks, to be bold, to allow my faith to push me to be uncomfortable for the sake of others and eternity."

Obedience

Commit to somehow making today unique. Own the fact that God can use you and wants to use you. Look for one opportunity to change a situation around you (whether it be big or small).

SOME PURPOSES IN PRAYER ARE ONLY ACCOMPLISHED WHEN WE *pray as one*

truth 10

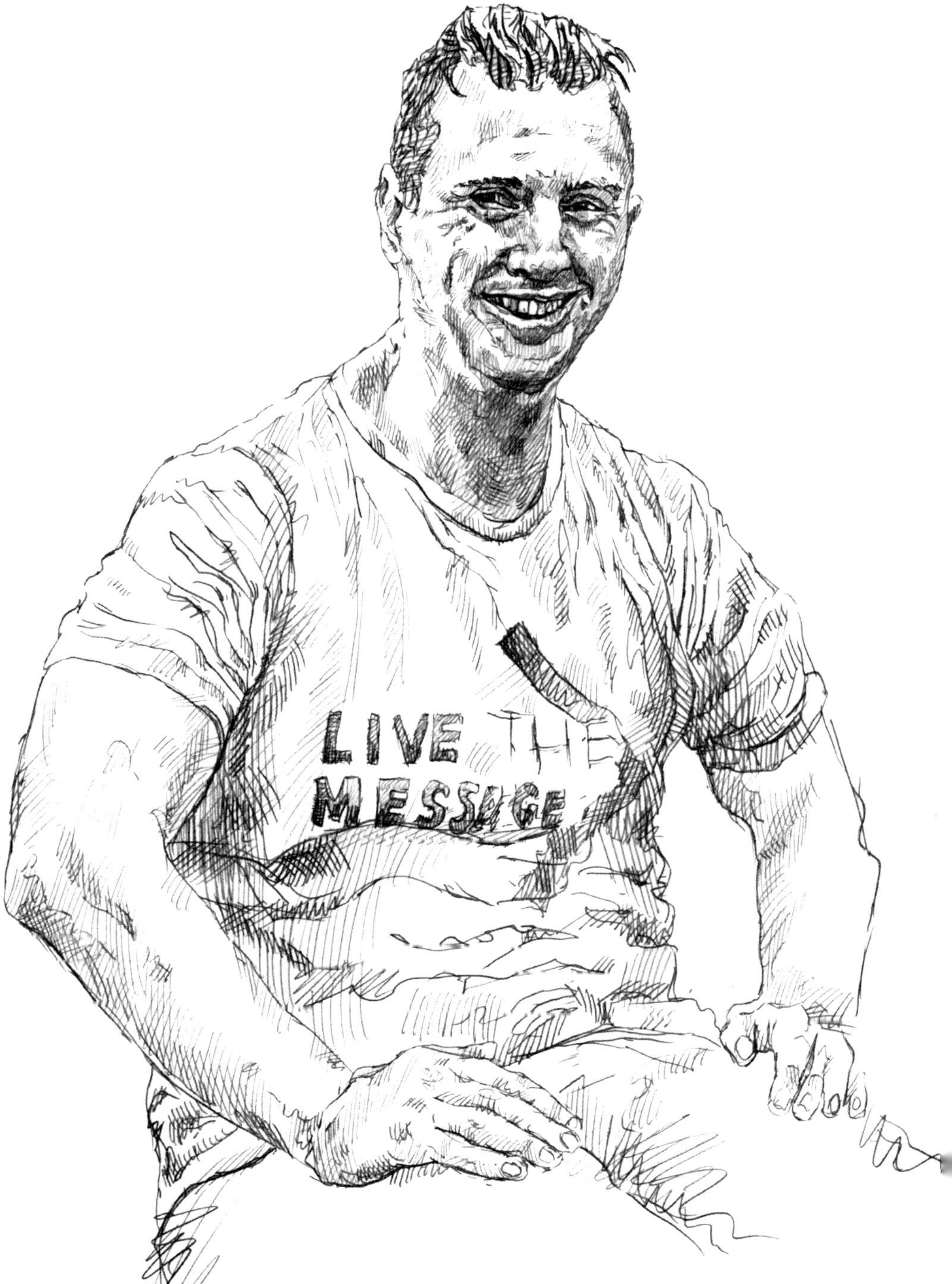
LIVE THE
MESSAGE

24
WHY WE PRAY TOGETHER

The Word

Psalm 67, John 17:20-26, Acts 4:23-37, Acts 16:25-40

God calls us to do some heavy lifting. Some things cannot be lifted alone or in isolation. God calls us to go after some of the big things together.

The heavy lifting of prayer is done in the trenches of corporate prayer. Any time two or three gather in the name of Jesus seeking to be obedient to Him, it is referred to as corporate prayer. And corporate prayer is needed in our generation to break through the opposition and assault of the enemy.

God used Aaron and Hur to hold the hands of Moses (Exodus 17:8-16) so that Israel could overcome the Amalekites. God used the seven priests, and the shout of all the people under Joshua's leadership to overcome the fortress of Jericho (Joshua 6:1-27). And He used a collective of repentant people turning and seeking the face of God to turn the heart of an entire nation (2 Chronicles 7:14-18). This is His pattern, and we best not think we have graduated from these basic ways of God moving in a generation.

The modern church has over-emphasized individualism to the point that God's work amongst a collective of people is almost foreign. Consumer Christianity has resulted in isolation. Prayer with others can seem too slow and bulky for our already busy lives. What's the point of taking time to pray together when we can figure things out on our own? The truth is, some things just will not happen until we learn to pray together. The process of submitting one to another and collectively submitting to the leading of the Lord, gives way to a fresh move of God, marked by the love of God. At the heart of the love of God is the preference of another over oneself.

Prayer

"Teach me how to submit to others. Teach me what it means to pray in one accord with other believers. Give me a vision of what is possible when we humble ourselves together in prayer. I need You, Jesus."

Obedience

Take time to talk to someone about this truth. Talk about the dynamics that keep us from praying together. Also talk about God's potential in our city and nation if we took this seriously.

25
THE POWER OF UNITY

The Word

Psalm 47, Ephesians 4:1-16, 1 John 4:7-21

Unity is not uniformity. Instead, unity more resembles the beauty of harmony than the sameness of uniformity. Unity isn't talked about much today because it's either seen as powerless relativism or as mass conformity. What is unity?

Jesus is one with the Father and calls us to be one with each other. But this oneness isn't uniformity. The Son of God is distinct from the Father. The Holy Spirit is distinct from the Son. But the three persons of the Godhead are in perfect unity. They are never in competition with each other. They have a singleness of mind, purpose, and will. The majesty of God can be seen in His complex unity. He is revealed to us through unique personalities (Father, Son, and Holy Spirit), yet functions as the One and Only God of creation and redemption.

As Christ followers, we are ushered into a spiritual relationship with other believers, a complex unity on its own level. We each have distinct personalities, relationships with God, stories in God, roles to play, but we are called to function together as one with a singleness of mind, purpose, and will. Sadly, this is a distant concept for the modern church. The power in the church has been sapped by preferences and styles. We divide and criticize. We give room for pride and posturing that pretends to have the corner on the kingdom.

I believe God is simplifying the church. I've noticed a greater call back to the simple gospel, authentic Christianity, and the power of the

Holy Spirit. I believe this refreshingly simple call back to the basics of New Testament Christianity will result in a unity in the church like we've never seen before. May we be in one accord.

Prayer

"Lord, help me begin to prefer others over myself. Help me to see other believers in through a lens of your love. May we experience in our day, what Jesus called for, that we may be one."

Obedience

Take time to dismantle any critical spirit in your heart toward other believers. Make a commitment to Jesus to keep the simple gospel in the forefront as we see a wave of believers do the same.

PRAYER IS *action* IN THE KINGDOM

truth 11

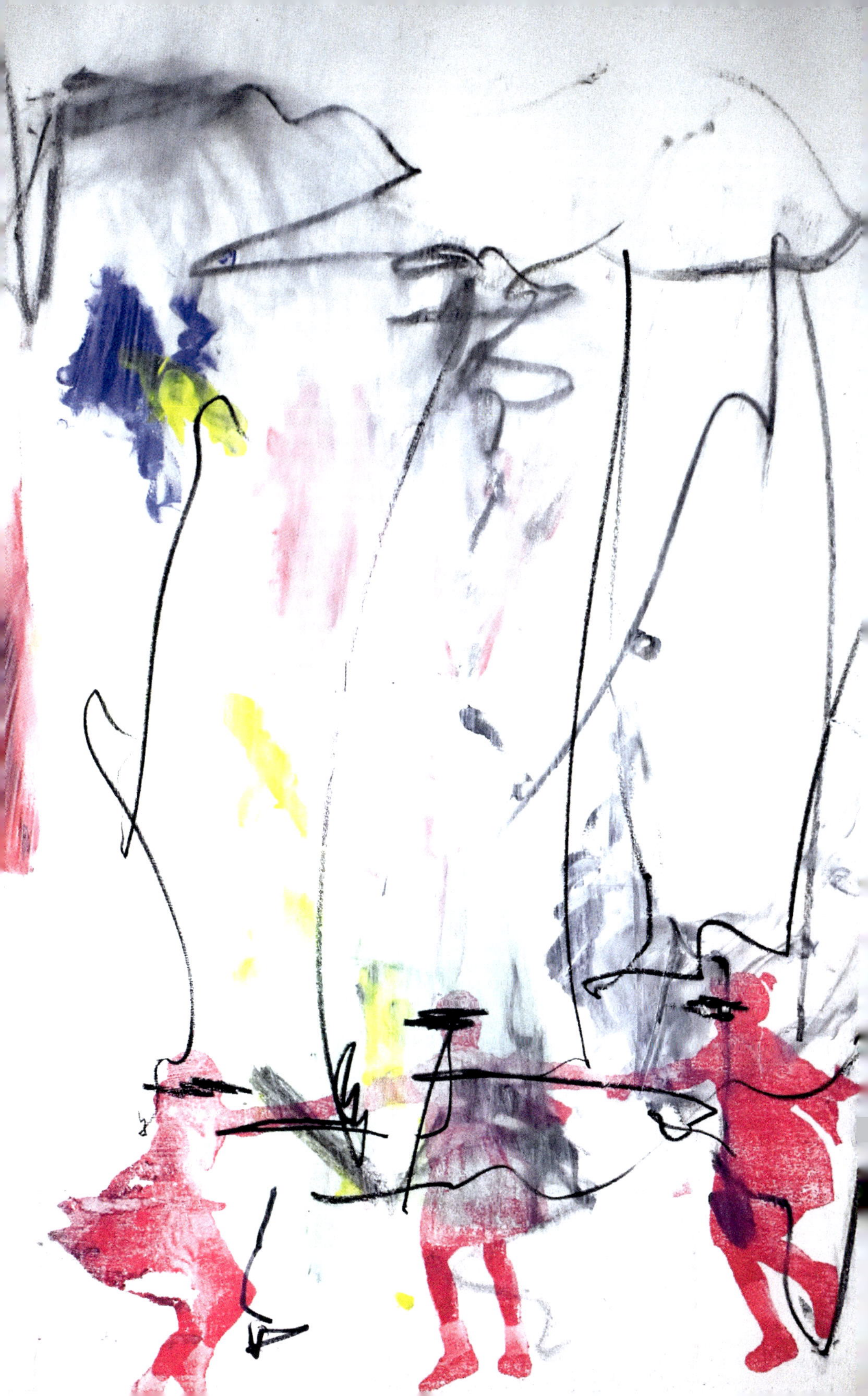

26
AN INVITATION FOR ACTION

The Word

Psalm 91, Matthew 26:36-46, Ephesians 6:10-20

Prayer is not idle or passive. Prayer is action in the Kingdom. Prayer is how Jesus began his sprint of earthly ministry—He went into the wilderness to pray. Prayer is how Jesus led Himself to give His life on the cross—He went into the garden to pray with His friends. For Jesus, prayer was not filler or an afterthought, it was the doorway into action.

We need to change our mindset regarding prayer. If we are bored in prayer, we've got it wrong. Jesus equates prayer with "watching". Prayer is how we alert our spirit to the real influences at play. Jesus commands us to pray with our spiritual eyes wide open so we can begin to recognize what's at stake. When we pray, our spiritual senses are awakened to the realities at work.

In our hyperactive world, prayer can be exalted to its place of premier action. The enemy is numbing our spiritual senses with an overdose of media, screens, and constant noise. But there's a battle waging that we are oblivious to. Jesus calls us to "put on the whole armor of God, so we can stand against the schemes of the devil" (Ephesians 6:11). Armor isn't needed if we're sitting idly. Armor is needed for action.

God is calling us back to the ways of His Kingdom when we do only what we see the Father doing and seek first His righteousness. He is giving us an invitation for real action that mimics His lifestyle of prayer that leads to outward action.

Prayer

"Today I choose to take action and seek You, God. You have called me to 'watch and pray' and I desire to be obedient. Help me be alert and attentive to everything at stake. I need You, Jesus!"

Obedience

Pray a bold prayer for God to open your eyes to the action of prayer. Reset your mind to begin to understand prayer as action and nothing less.

27
JESUS OUR EXAMPLE

The Word

Psalm 31, Hebrews 4:14-5:10

Jesus, Son of God, Savior of the world, prayed with "loud cries and tears." He prayed with an intensity that should make us scratch our heads. He said He is one with Father. Yet He was compelled to pray with a genuine passion that communicated that prayer matters.

Jesus provides us with an example of the action of prayer. For Jesus, prayer was not a wishful experiment or a duty, it was His demonstration of dependence. Prayer was His perfect expression of submission to the will of the Father. Jesus prayed as though everything depended on it, because as the Son of God in perfect relationship with the Father, everything did. Prayer is action.

God wants to teach us a lot about the things accomplished in prayer. There is not a single instance in the Bible of prayer being described as a mind-numbing ritual. Instead, prayer is the means by which things are "loosed in heaven" (Matthew 16:19), mountains are cast into the sea (Matthew 21:21), the sick are healed (Mark 16:18), the hearts of kings are softened (Proverbs 21:1). Jesus knew it all and knew that He was demonstrating to His disciples to come, what was possible in prayer.

Let's look to Jesus' life as a reason to passionately pursue God in prayer. Let's root out all apathy and excuses for passivity. Prayer is action.

Prayer

"Oh God, help me root out all apathy in my life. I want to come alive to the fullness of what prayer means in this life. I want to jump in and be a part of what You are doing. Give me eyes to see the urgency of this moment."

Obedience

Take time today to declare the significant promises described above regarding faith-filled prayer. Don't leave your time of declaration until there is a shift in your conviction of the action filled sense of prayer.

EVERYONE CAN HAVE A *secret place* OF PRAYER

truth 12

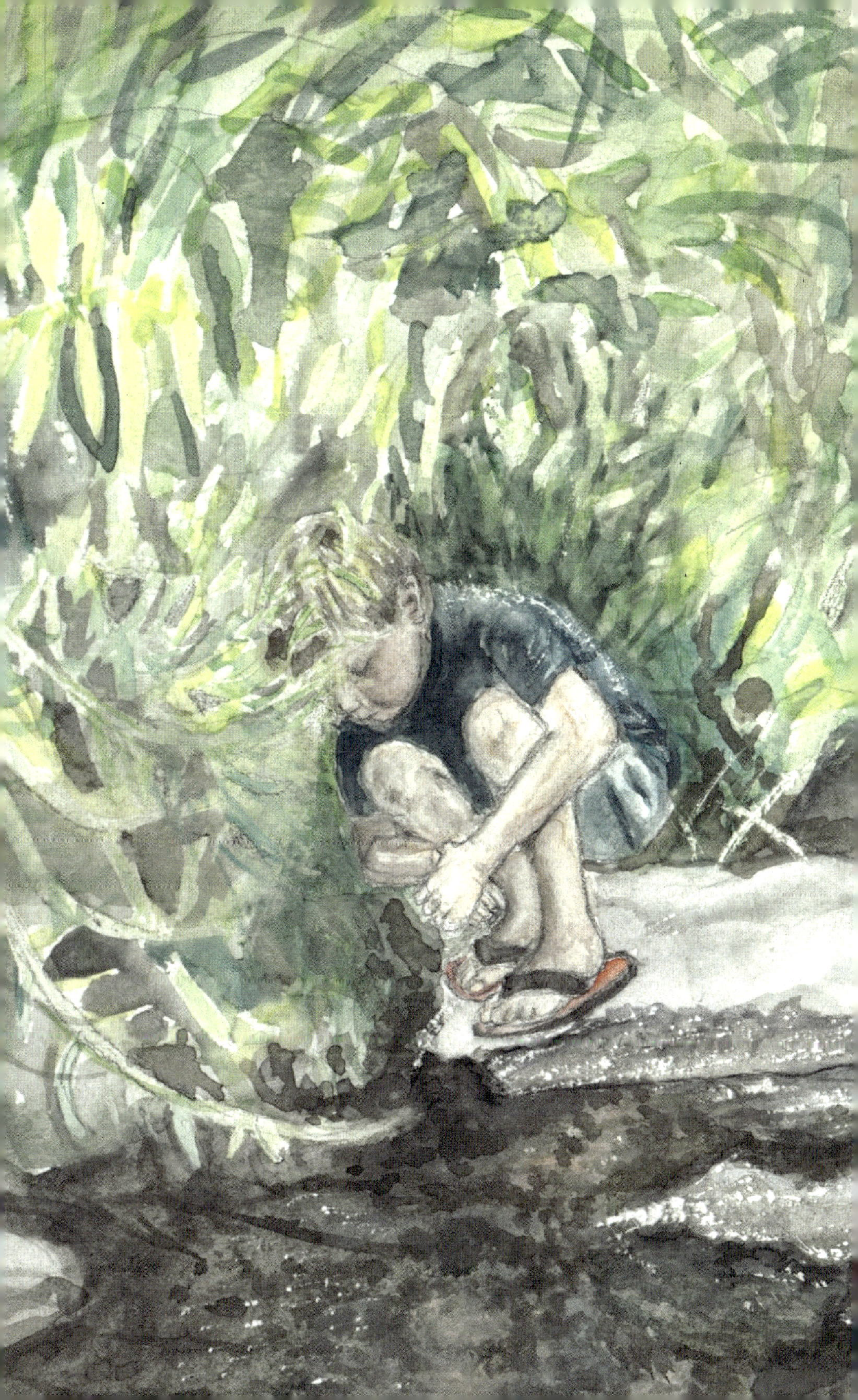

28
PRAYING IN THE SPIRIT

The Word

Psalm 62, Matthew 6:5-14, 1 Corinthians 14

Paul says that when he prays in tongues, he is praying in the spirit (1 Corinthians 14:14). Therefore, Paul defines one way in which we pray in the spirit. When Scripture tells us to keep "praying at all times in the spirit" (Ephesians 6:18 or Jude 20), it gives us the challenge of praying in our prayer language often. This is something no one else can do for you and you get to uniquely express to God.

God has created an intimate opportunity for every disciple to express themselves to the Lord in prayer. If you have placed your faith in Jesus Christ as Savior, then the Holy Spirit lives in you. Praying in the spirit gives voice to the Spirit of God in you, to pray in perfect alignment with the will of God. And when we understand that, it makes sense that we would not know what we are praying when we pray in tongues. This way of praying surrenders the most defiant part of our body—our tongue—to God in prayer. Often when we pray in our native language (which we should), our own will and prejudices get in the way. But when we surrender even our tongues to God for His Spirit to pray in us, we become vessels of the miraculous.

Paul said he prayed in tongues more than all of the Corinthians (1 Corinthians 14:18). And some scholars believe the most literal translation means that he prayed in tongues more than all of the Corinthians believers combined. But he is taking about private tongues. He prays in the spirit in private more than all of the believers. Which for me, begs the question, how much more should I prioritize prayer in the spirit? There must be more to this than I have known. It makes me desire more of God and a greater intimacy to trust Him with my tongue.

Prayer

"Today Lord I surrender even my tongue to You. I know often my words don't align with Your will. I want to walk in relationship with You like never before. I desire greater intimacy. I desire You!"

Obedience

If you have been baptized in the Spirit, spend time today just praying in your prayer language. If you have not been baptized in the Holy Spirit, pray to receive this promised gift (read Acts 1:8).

_____

_____

_____

_____

_____

_____

_____

_____

_____

29
THE SECRET PLACE

The Word

Psalm 9, Matthew 6:5-15, Jude

Jesus says, "When you pray, go into your room and shut the door and pray to your Father who is in secret" (Matthew 6:6). There is a secret place of prayer just for you and God.

When Jesus said this, He was contending against hypocritical religious elites that showcased their prayers in public places to gain the respect and adoration of people. That type of prayer is powerless. There is no purpose in prayer performances. Jesus said, "they have received their reward (Matthew 6:5)." Their reward was as short lived and simple as the praise or opinion of others.

We shut ourselves in the secret place and cry out to God where there is no posturing or pretending. It's just you and God. Jesus says, "And your Father who sees in secret will reward you (Matthew 6:6)." This is truly powerful prayer—prayer in the secret place. It's from our position in the secret place that God really does work through the prayers of His people. He rewards us with all of the fruit of walking with Him, but He also rewards us with glimpses into His fulfilled promises.

Every follower of Jesus needs to find this secret place with God for themselves. No one can do it for you. Don't delay.

Prayer

"Jesus, thank You inviting me into the secret place. Thank You for calling me *by name. I choose to respond. Teach me Your ways and teach me how to pray. I want to walk with You in real intimacy."*

Obedience

Take time today to discover "the secret place" as Jesus described in Matthew 6. Find a place where you can get completely alone with God. It's there that you can cry out to God and discover the power of the secret place with God.

30
EXPERIENCE IS NECESSARY

The Word

Deuteronomy 10:12-22, Joshua 1:1-9, Psalm 34, 1 Corinthians 2

A.W. Tozer said, "Whatever else it embraces, true Christian experience must always include a genuine encounter with God. Without this, religion is but a shadow, a reflection of reality, a cheap copy of an original once enjoyed by someone else of whom we have heard (Tozer, pg. 10)[1]."

In Christianity, experience is necessary. Christianity is not a religion meant to be confined to a lecture hall, classroom, or chapel. Christianity is meant to truly impact our lives. Jesus gave His life so that every aspect of our lives can be changed, transformed, and redeemed. That's why this devotional was designed to give opportunities for response and obedience. Knowing about something and experiencing something first-hand make for completely different end results.

Everyone can know God through prayer, but prayer must be given space to be experienced. Prayer can't be just talked about or understood intellectually. Eventually (and the sooner the better), it must be experienced. This guided journey in prayer was meant to catalyze just that, the experience of prayer. I pray what was sparked in this season will result in a long-term lifestyle of prayer.

Prayer

"Lord, give me grace to press in and truly know You for myself. I don't want to

---

[1] Tozer, A.W. God's Pursuit of Man. Wingspread Publishers, Camp Hill, PA. 1950

rely on anyone else's knowledge or experience. I want to know You first hand. Thank You for drawing me to You."

Obedience

Today reflect on the major differences between knowing about something intellectually and knowing something firsthand through experience.

Appendix

Promises of God

"The promises of God are 'Yes' in Christ" • *2 Corinthians 1:20*

- If my people who are called by my name humble themselves, and pray and seek my face and turn from their wicked ways, then I will hear from heaven and will forgive their sin and heal their land *(2 Chronicles 7:14)*.

- Even though I walk through the valley of the shadow of death, I will fear no evil, for you are with me; your rod and your staff, they comfort me *(Psalm 23:4)*.

- When the righteous cry for help, the Lord hears and delivers them out of all their troubles *(Psalm 34:17)*.

- Delight yourself in the Lord, and he will give you the desires of your heart *(Psalm 37:4)*.

- For you, O Lord, are good and forgiving, abounding in steadfast love to all who call upon you *(Psalm 86:5)*.

- They who wait for the Lord shall renew their strength; they shall mount up with wings like eagles; they shall run and not be weary; they shall walk and not faint *(Isaiah 40:31)*.

- ...Fear not, for I am with you; be not dismayed, for I am your God; I will strengthen you, I will help you, I will uphold you with my righteous right hand *(Isaiah 41:10)*.

- The Lord is good, a stronghold in the day of trouble; he knows those who take refuge in him *(Nahum 1:7)*.

- But seek first the kingdom of God and his righteousness, and all these things will be added to you *(Matthew 6:33)*.
- If you then, who are evil, know how to give good gifts to your children, how much more will your Father who is in heaven give good things to those who ask him *(Matthew 7:11)*.
- Therefore I tell you, whatever you ask in prayer, believe that you have received it, and it will be yours *(Mark 11:24)*.
- So if the Son sets you free, you will be free indeed *(John 8:36)*.
- Christ received from the Father the promise of the Holy Spirit *(Acts 2:33)*; the promise is to you and to your children *(Acts 2:39)*.
- Do not be anxious about anything, but in everything by prayer and supplication with thanksgiving let your requests be made known to God. And the peace of God, which surpasses all understanding, will guard your hearts and your minds in Christ Jesus *(Philippians 4:6–7)*.
- And my God will supply every need of yours according to his riches in glory in Christ Jesus *(Philippians 4:19)*.
- …The promise of entering His rest remains *(Hebrews 4:1)*.
- If any of you lacks wisdom, let him ask God, who gives generously to all without reproach, and it will be given him *(James 1:5)*.
- Is anyone among you sick? Let him call for the elders of the church, and let them pray over him, anointing him with oil in the name of the Lord. And the prayer of faith will save the one who is sick, and the Lord will raise him up *(James 5:14–15)*.
- Submit yourselves therefore to God. Resist the devil, and he will flee from you *(James 4:7)*.
- If we confess our sins, he is faithful and just to forgive us our sins and to cleanse us from all unrighteousness *(1 John 1:9)*.

Image Index

Holzbauer, Paige 5, 14*, 20, 24*, 30*, 31, 36*, 37, 42*, 54, 58*, 66*, 78-79* (top), 84*, 85, 90*, 102

Jinkins, Robert 19, 43, 67, 78-79 (bottom), 102

Nickerson, Tayler 59

Savage, Amy 15, 25, 49, 50*, 51, 65, 72*, 73, 91

*= background image

Acknowledgements

I want to take space to communicate gratitude to a number of people that made this project possible. First of all, I want to thank my wife, Tanya, for being my closest prayer companion and prayer backing as we have continually stepped out and trusted God. I want to thank Tony Meyer, Nicole Barnes, and Riley Edwards for being amazing friends and leaders, and helping create capacity for projects like this. I want to thank Laura Saunders for her excellent attention to detail and for helping make this project be the best it could be through her editing skills. I want to give a huge thank you to Kayla Meyer for designing and formatting the interior of this book. And I want to thank Amy Savage for heading up the team of artists that really made this project something special.

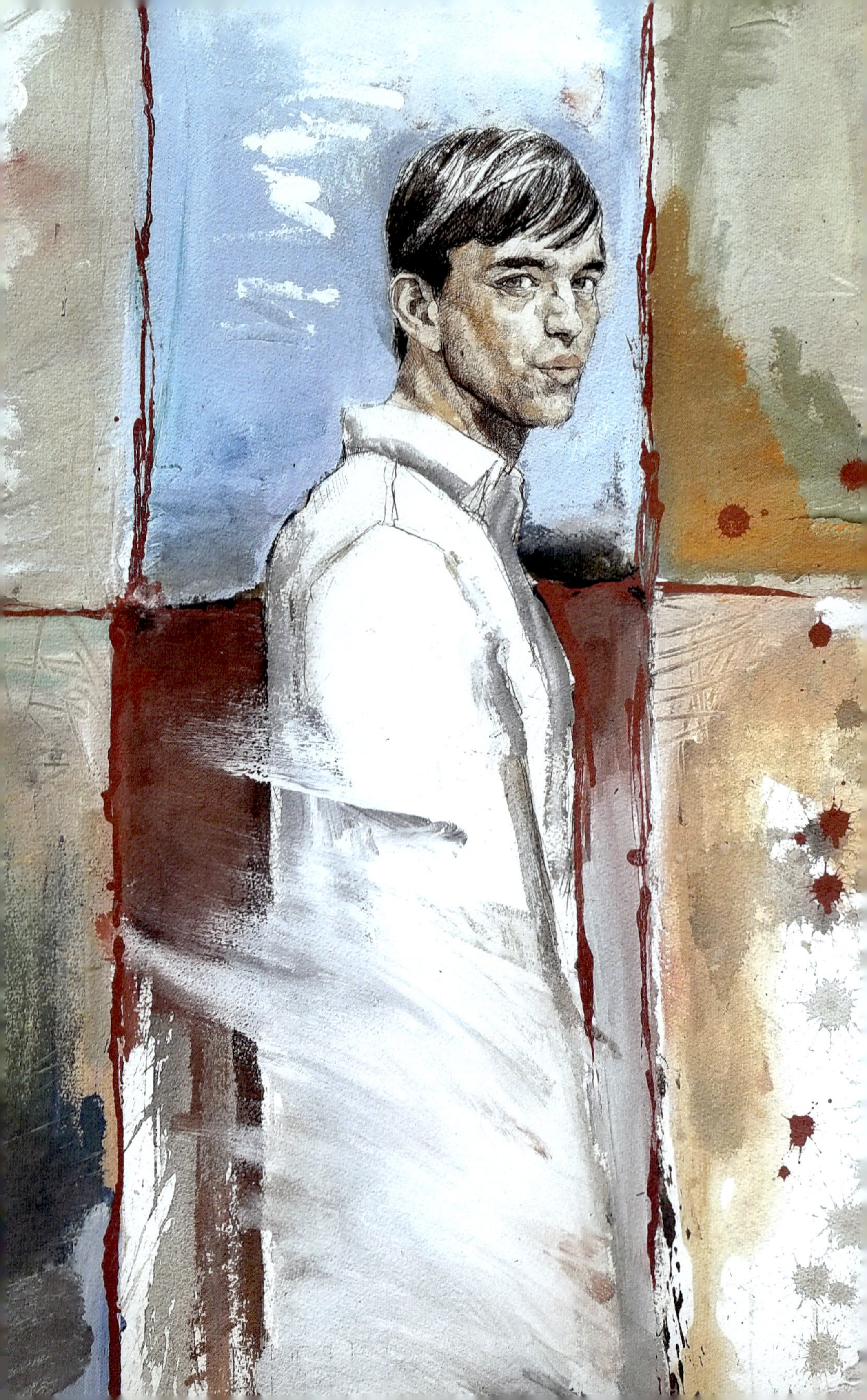

About the Author

Drew Meyer is the lead pastor at LifePointe Church in Ames, IA. Drew and his family moved to Ames in 2011 to start a campus ministry to Iowa State University. His love for Ames and the local expression of the church through LifePointe Church has only grown. His desire is to see the church live and experience the life-giving power of the message of Jesus. For more information, go to livethemessage.org or lifepointe.cc.

Prayer Journal

Date | Prayer Need

Prayer Journal

Date   Prayer Need

Made in the USA
Lexington, KY
19 December 2019